Broadway Christian Churc...
A Return to Virtue Reflections or...
Bell, James S.

P9-EEU-354

0000 2217

CL 1   2217
Bel   Bell, James S.
         A Return to Virtue

DATE DUE

PROPERTY OF
BROADWAY CHRISTIAN CHURCH LIBRARY
910 BROADWAY
FORT WAYNE, IN 46802

DEMCO

A RETURN TO

VIRTUE

REFLECTIONS
ON LIVING
WISELY

A RETURN TO
VIRTUE

REFLECTIONS
ON LIVING
WISELY

JAMES S. BELL, JR.
STAN CAMPBELL

PROPERTY OF
BROADWAY CHRISTIAN CHURCH LIBRARY
910 BROADWAY
FORT WAYNE, IN 46802

NORTHFIELD PUBLISHING
CHICAGO

© 1995 by
JAMES S. BELL, JR., AND
STAN CAMPBELL

All rights reserved. No part of this book may be reproduced in any form without permission in writing from the publisher, except in the case of brief quotations embodied in critical articles or reviews.

All Scripture quotations, unless indicated, are taken from the *Holy Bible: New International Version®*. NIV®. Copyright © 1973, 1978, 1984 International Bible Society. Used by permission of Zondervan Publishing House. All rights reserved.

The definition of each virtue is taken from *Webster's Encyclopedic Unabridged Dictionary of the English Language*. New York: Random House, 1989. All rights reserved.

ISBN: 1-881273-04-0

1 3 5 7 9 10 8 6 4 2

Printed in the United States of America

*To my wife Margaret,
who for me is the epitome
of a life of virtue*
—J. S. B.

CONTENTS

Acknowledgments 9

To the Reader 11

Character 14

Chastity 20

Compassion 24

Conscience 30

Contentment 34

Courage 40

Courtesy 46

Diligence 52

Faith 56

Forgiveness 62

Friendship 66

Frugality 72

Generosity 76

Gentleness 82

Goodness 86

Gratitude 92

Honesty 96

Honor 102

Hope 108

Humility 114

Integrity 120

Justice	124
Kindness	130
Love	136
Loyalty	142
Morality	146
Obedience	150
Patience	154
Perseverance	160
Prudence	166
Purpose	172
Responsibility	176
Reverence	182
Self-control	186
Self-knowledge	190
Self-sacrifice	194
Service	198
Simplicity	202
Sincerity	206
Temperance	210
Tolerance	214
Trust	218
Truth	222
Virtue	228
Wisdom	234
Work	240

ACKNOWLEDGMENTS

*T*hanks go first and foremost to the visionary publishing committee at Moody Press. Their emphasis on practicality and application helped us comtemporize the inestimable wisdom of the ages. Kudos as well to the Moody Press editorial staff, who clarified the nuances of virtuous living. We won't neglect to applaud the efforts of Kelly Cluff, who assisted with the definitions. And, finally, thanks to our family members, who relinquished valuable time in anticipation of learning more of the art of living wisely.

THE AUTHORS

TO THE READER

◆

*U*ntil recently it seemed as if the word *virtue* was suffering the same fate as other unfairly maligned words: puritan, virgin, and moralist. Yet, suddenly, inexplicably, virtue is relevant and even welcomed. It's found in management books, self-help books, even health books. It's on the best-seller list. Why? Perhaps it is because some people think that it just might be the missing piece of the puzzle, the key to putting everything back together that we seem to be losing—strong families and communities, a meaningful education, a significant career, a personal faith, and a high individual purpose in life.

These are lofty goals, but as we look back many of us think we were once on the right road and somehow virtuous living was a part of it. Others (perhaps younger) feel they were never taught in-depth about virtue and are missing a great secret.

Perhaps we've all had an overdose of the "me generation," sexual revolution, or situation ethics. Regardless of the reason, we're rediscovering that virtue rules, that it works in everyday living. There are no free lunches or short cuts to the things that matter most. Living for merely selfish reasons will never satisfy us.

We want to be known as caring, giving, full of integrity, and (dare I say it?) good people. But to be the latter instead of the former kind of person we need to employ sacrifice, diligence, and be unpopular at times. More than that, when it comes to the many virtues or character qualities we all agree on, we need to seek to understand, reflect, apply, even study.

That is why we wrote this book. Studying is no fun when you have to start from scratch or interpret everything on your own. So we've compiled samples from the wisdom of the ages on the character qualities that count by some great people who believed what they said and at least tried to live it. Then we've tried to relate it to your life and the world you live in to blow away the dust and mystery.

Coincidentally (or not) these people through the centuries agree pretty closely on the rules of the game of life. We may live in a high-tech world by comparison, but our desires, worries, conduct, and purposes are quite similar to theirs. They may have some answers for us that have been recently buried in our brave new world.

Sometimes less principled people reinvent or water down the meaning of these virtues over time, so definitions are included to keep us honest. Maybe you'll be shocked to see how far we've veered off course, or perhaps you'll feel good about your past achievements. But the purpose of this book is to help you improve today.

In the selection on courtesy found within, it says we can do a lot of small things in no time to improve our lives and others' as well. Character development gradually becomes a habit. You work on one quality at a time, just as we exhibit one per page.

Finally, remember that the words of these sages carry more weight than ours. Just as the virtues are back in style, we hope that the reading of the great classics will be also. Give them a try.

At the least, we hope you come away sold on virtuous living, with a desire to grow in some aspect of virtue that will in turn be a benefit to others. If so, the authors will increase in the virtue of gratitude, and writing this book will have been worthwhile.

***C**haracter; N. the aggregate of features and traits that form the apparent individual nature of some person or thing; qualities of honesty, courage, or the like; integrity; reputation; good repute; an account of the moral qualities, ethical standards, principles; the distinctive qualities which make one recognizable as a person differentiated from others*

THE FLAW THAT FORMED THE CAMEL'S BACK

Character is simply habit long continued.
Plutarch

*I*n Rudyard Kipling's *Just So Stories*, he explains in mythical fashion how the camel got its hump. It seems that the camel would not work with the other animals. When asked to help the horses, dogs, and oxen, he would reply with a "Humph!" So the animals complained to a genie, who appealed to the camel personally. But the camel kept responding with a huffy "Humph!" until the genie literally gave him a "humph" on his back—allowing him to go longer without water so that he could catch up on his work.

Our habits can become literal characteristics. If we wish to create a pleasing character rather than an unappealing one, we need to closely examine our habits. What begins as an occasional slip quickly becomes a bad habit—and can further escalate into a permanent character flaw.

Do you ever catch yourself letting the quality of your work slide just a bit? Do you tune your ears to gossip more than you used to? Is pride creeping up on you? Is your kindness in shorter supply?

Your habits eventually become your character, so take a lesson from the camel. Eliminate your negative qualities now—or, like the camel, you may carry them for a lifetime. The positive qualities of virtuous living will get you over the hump.

A BAD TRADE

*Character is always lost when a high ideal is
sacrificed on the altar of conformity and popularity.*

Anonymous

*B*usiness consultants describe a common phenomenon in
many organizations. A young person is hired who has an
instinctive ability to motivate people by treating them with
respect. The employees in turn produce well for the new supervisor. Naturally, this person quickly climbs the corporate ladder
and is pegged as upper management material. But that's where
"the change" often occurs.

As a lower-level employee, the person succeeded because of
his or her unique outlook and high ideals. Yet once the leap is
made into management, conformity suddenly takes precedence. Dress, language, and even ideas quickly adapt to those
of other executives. The most tragic result is that the manager
forsakes a previous high ideal of the potential and value of people in exchange for "bottom line" concerns and personal advancement.

There's nothing wrong with conformity or popularity. The
problem is in sacrificing high ideals to get there, for the loss of
character is almost never regained. After Lancelot slept with
Guinevere, the glory of Camelot quickly came to an end. When
Judas betrayed Jesus, a crucifixion and suicide followed within
hours.

If you don't want the insurmountable task of trying to re-
assemble your good character, the secret is to do whatever it
takes to keep from sacrificing it in the first place.

CHARACTER

WATCH FOR HIDDEN CAMERAS

Character is what you are in the dark.
Dwight L. Moody

"*Q*uick! While nobody's looking!"

Do you recall these words from childhood? They usually accompany a challenge, such as swiping cookies from the jar, smoking a cigarette, shoplifting candy from a store, drinking a beer, testing a sheet/parachute from an upper window, or some other illicit activity. If you weren't the one chiding someone else to attempt such things, you probably received your share of challenges.

Yes, kids will be kids. But unfortunately, some of us never outgrow the mind-set that almost any activity is OK as long as no one is looking. We laugh at programs such as "Candid Camera" that show how people behave when they don't know they're being watched. But if we are wise, we also see the potential tragedies of a life based on trying to "get by" with whatever we can.

No matter how good we get at spotting the hidden cameras or seeing the prying eyes that gaze in our direction, no one is good enough to avoid the self-awareness of the shallowness of such a lifestyle. The cameras of one's own eyes, heart, and conscience never shut down. When we lie in bed at night, we know who we are.

Character is what you are in the dark. Someone might switch on the lights at any moment and yell "Surprise!" Will you be the same person you pretend to be in the light?

CHARACTER

Character is simply habit long continued.
Plutarch

*Character is always lost when a high ideal is
sacrificed on the altar of conformity and popularity.*
Anonymous

Character is what you are in the dark.
Dwight L. Moody

*C*hastity; *Adj. not having engaged in unlawful sexual intercourse; virtuous; free from obscenity; decent; pure in style; subdued; simple; unaffected; unadorned; neat; classic; elegant*

VIRTUE IS MORE THAN SKIN DEEP

Be warm, but pure; be amorous, but be chaste.
Lord Byron

*C*onsider how much money people spend each year to look good for others—cosmetics, hair stylists, brand-name fashions, health clubs, athletic equipment, diets, workout videos, specialized books/tapes/magazines, cosmetic surgery, and so forth. Millions more are spent on advertising to convince you that you need terrific-smelling hair, minty breath, and blinding-white teeth.

People want to look good for different reasons. Some want to look healthy. Others hope to get noticed. But some people hope to "get lucky," and that is where problems arise.

Chastity is the virtue that spices up relationships without endangering them. When chastity is assured by two people of different genders, they can have the privilege of feeling "warm" and "amorous." Walls can come down, and they can be more vulnerable with each other. The rites of flirtation can take their course and romance can blossom. If not, they can still share of themselves and reveal passions regarding other matters. There is no fear that their signals will be misread.

Lord Byron makes wise distinctions. We need to move beyond superficial *physical* allures and become attractive through *interpersonal* ones. We can seek out warm, pure, loving relationships—but we should always know where to draw the line. The adolescent thrill of being chased can be replaced by the security of being chaste. The two may sound alike, but there's a world of difference.

FOLLOW YOUR PASSIONS

*The essence of chastity is not the
suppression of lust, but the total
orientation of one's life towards a goal.*
Dietrich Bonhoeffer

*T*here are two ways to approach chastity. The more common
one is the "just say no" approach, often backed with scare tactics (AIDS statistics, threats of other sexual diseases and dis-
graces, and so on). Yet even when people dwell on "No sex. No
sex. No sex" they spend just as much time thinking "sex" as
they do thinking "no."

We all have a desire to feel passionate. Unfortunately, passion
has been linked with sex so frequently that the two may appear
synonymous. So a second approach to chastity is suggested by
Bonhoeffer—find a more worthwhile channel for passion.

Without an overriding life goal, we're left to deal with whatever we feel at the moment. Our needs for a positive self-image
and acceptance can team up with our desires for pleasure and
immediate gratification. If unchecked, this can result in powerful temptations when opportunities arise for sexual contact.

We need to better define other goals into which we can—and
should—channel our passion (one's spouse, children, work,
hobbies, spiritual growth). With a principled life goal before
us, we become more disciplined to make progress toward it.
We make sacrifices. Chastity begins to make sense and fits into
a general commitment to virtuous living.

Passion and chastity make a good combination. If you can
have both, why settle for one or the other?

CHASTITY

Be warm, but pure; be amorous, but be chaste.
Lord Byron

The essence of chastity is not the suppression of lust,
but the total orientation of one's life towards a goal.
Dietrich Bonhoeffer

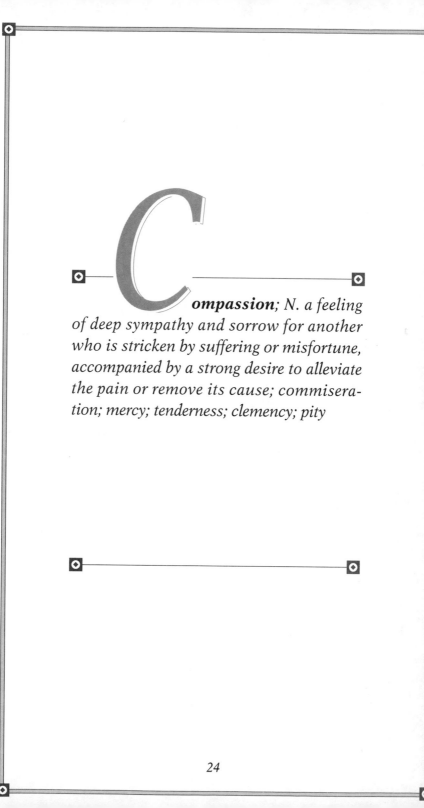

***C**ompassion; N. a feeling of deep sympathy and sorrow for another who is stricken by suffering or misfortune, accompanied by a strong desire to alleviate the pain or remove its cause; commiseration; mercy; tenderness; clemency; pity*

THE WOE MUST GO ON

Pity is best taught by fellowship in woe.
Samuel Taylor Coleridge

*D*ozens of movies use essentially the same format: two people of extreme opposite viewpoints are forced to spend time with each other, and they gradually come to understand and appreciate one another's views. We've had the black driver and the old-fashioned white woman, the teenaged boy and his older and wiser karate instructor, the Detroit cop and the Beverly Hills police, and Captain Kirk and any number of alien life forms.

As the "fellowship" between the characters increases, so does their understanding of each other. And so it is whenever we spend time with others. What Coleridge called "pity" we might better translate as "empathy"—the ability to relate to other people from our shared experiences and emotions.

When your own life is going smoothly, it's hard to care about those in "woe." You don't want to hear about anyone else's depressing news. But when *you* face a personal loss, you suddenly discover how valuable a friend is.

The hard way to learn pity is to wait until your next crisis and then seek help. A better way is to open your eyes, your ears, and your heart to the hurting people around you. Fellowship with them in their woe until they are able to join you in your joy. Then, when your own time of woe comes along, those people will be strong enough to return the favor.

GIVE A JUDGE ENOUGH ROPE . . .

*We hand folks over to God's
mercy, and show none ourselves.*
George Eliot

*I*t's too bad that the job market for hanging judges has pretty much closed up during the last century. So many of us seem to have all the right credentials. As long as we could utter that final disclaimer, "And may God have mercy on your soul," we could heartlessly send miscreants off to meet their maker.

Maybe your heartlessness doesn't go to quite that extreme, yet it seems that mercy and compassion are disappearing characteristics in most relationships today. You don't have to talk to many people before you'll find one who is harboring grudges that go back for years—if not generations. We take major offense at minor infractions. We insist that people treat us with respect, even if we have to scream and shout so they'll understand us.

But before we pursue lives as free-lance judges, we would be wise to remember that there are rules for judges. One of the guidelines that Jesus provided is this: "In the same way you judge others, you will be judged, and with the measure you use, it will be measured to you" (Matthew 7:2).

What if we could count on only as much compassion and forgiveness from God that we show toward others? Be thankful that God has mercy on our souls—and then pass some of it on to others!

COME, PASSION

Compassion will cure more sins than condemnation.
Henry Ward Beecher

*D*o we really need to be reminded that we can catch more flies with honey than with vinegar? Apparently so. It's something most people profess to know and believe, yet from their actions it's difficult to tell.

We've all seen good-cop/bad-cop scenes in movies. We know that the harsh and condemning cop never gets the confession. It's always the patient and compassionate one who convinces the suspect to cooperate. Personal experience tells us it's not overbearing and demanding bosses who get us to do our best work. But we'll go out of our way for leaders who genuinely care about us.

So, if we know all these things, why do we yell at our kids or spouses when they need hugs instead? Why would we rather get even when offended instead of letting it go and finding peace? Why do we point out others' mistakes rather than trying to understand their circumstances and shortcomings? Why do we condemn ourselves for our mistakes instead of understanding that we are only human?

Condemnation contends, "You're no good, and you'll suffer the consequences." Compassion replies, "Of course you make mistakes, but you'll do better next time." If we first develop a passion for compassion, relationships will grow stronger. When that happens, problems between ourselves and others seem to take care of themselves.

COMPASSION

Pity is best taught by fellowship in woe.
Samuel Taylor Coleridge

We hand folks over to God's mercy,
and show none ourselves.
George Eliot

Compassion will cure more sins than condemnation.
Henry Ward Beecher

PROPERTY OF
BROADWAY CHRISTIAN CHURCH LIBRARY
910 BROADWAY
FORT WAYNE, IN 46802

Conscience; N. the sense of what is right or wrong in one's conduct or motives, impelling one toward right action; the complex of ethical and moral principles that controls or inhibits the actions or thoughts of an individual; an inhibiting sense of what is prudent; self-knowledge; conscientiousness; strict and reverential observance

IN GOOD CONSCIENCE

The only guide to a man is his conscience; the only shield to his memory is the rectitude and sincerity of his actions.
Sir Winston Churchill

*D*o you think Churchill's quote is just another way of saying, "Let your conscience be your guide"? Not exactly. Many people who use the conscience-as-guide argument do so to justify actions that are blatantly wrong. Their defense is, "It might be wrong for you, but if I don't feel guilty about it, it's OK for me."

Your definition makes a difference. Webster defines *conscience* as, "The sense or consciousness of the moral goodness or blameworthiness of one's own conduct, intentions, or character together with a feeling or obligation to do right or be good."

According to both Webster and Churchill, conscience involves not only *knowing* the difference between right and wrong but also *desiring* to do good. By this definition, conscience makes an excellent guide. But it is a guide that does not allow for selfish pursuits considered harmful to self or others.

Many people learn too late that we need a shield for our memories. As we look back across our lives, we can experience great joy and contentment as we recall "rectitude" (moral integrity) and "sincerity of actions." Our present lives take on greater significance with such a past. But too often we grimace as we remember the mistakes we made by either ignoring or redefining *conscience*.

We all need guides in life. But if your conscience is going to be your guide, you'd better be sure you can trust where it's taking you.

A SENSIBLE CONSCIENCE

*Men will never do evil so fully and so happily
as when they do it for conscience' sake.*

Blaise Pascal

*H*ow were Nazi soldiers able to kill millions of Jews during the Holocaust? Why are Ku Klux Klan members willing to hate and persecute entire races of people? Do the individuals in these organizations think, *We are some of the most evil people on earth, so we have every right to commit senseless, heinous crimes?*

Not likely. In most cases, these people are convinced that they are serving a righteous cause. As soon as they make this mental assumption—erroneous though it may be—they can justify almost any act in the name of conscience.

We shouldn't get too self-righteous, because all of us are capable of altering our personal code of ethics under certain conditions. War is an example. But these conditions should be the rare exception rather than the rule.

A jug of brown, stinking water might be a relief to someone dying of thirst in the desert. But under normal conditions he would want to replace it with clear, fresh liquid. Similarly, we need to make a periodic check that we are acting from a clean conscience rather than one that has become clouded and impure.

And remember that acting out of a clear conscience is not enough in itself. Members of hate groups can have a clear conscience. So even when your conscience is clear, check regularly to be sure that your hands and heart are clean as well.

CONSCIENCE

*The only guide to a man is his conscience;
the only shield to his memory is the
rectitude and sincerity of his actions.*
Sir Winston Churchill

*Men will never do evil so fully and so happily
as when they do it for conscience' sake.*
Blaise Pascal

C*ontentment; N. the state or feeling of being contented;*
— Adj. satisfied with what one is or has: not wanting more or anything else; satisfied

DON'T BE FOOLED BY IMITATIONS

Contentment is natural wealth,
luxury is artificial poverty.

Socrates

S tories are told of gold-rush prospectors who thought they'd struck it rich. They whooped and hollered down to the assayer's office only to discover (to their dismay) that they were mining pyrite—"fool's gold." It looked valuable, but it wasn't worth much more than the dirt it had been dug out of.

Socrates pre-dated the gold rush by 2,300 years, but he had already realized that it is foolish to place too much value on things. Think about it. Would a genuine gold nugget in your hand generate more contentment than a chunk of pyrite? Not really.

Prospectors were some of the least contented people around. Many were hermits consumed by greed, suspicion, and secrecy. Real gold brought no more contentment than fool's gold.

The "golden" elements of contentment are intangible: a life well-lived; interfacing well with nature, others, self, and God; the ability to laugh. Material things—luxuries—are artificial attempts to generate a feeling that money can't buy.

We can choose to emulate Donald Trump or Mother Teresa— to pursue artificial luxury or natural wealth. If we contrast only the lifestyles, we lean one direction. But when we consider the lasting results, we might decide on the other.

CHECK BELONGINGS AT THE DOOR

*Godliness with contentment is great gain. For
we brought nothing into the world, and we
can take nothing out of it. But if we have
food and clothing, we will be content with that.*
The Apostle Paul, New Testament

*T*he common adaptation of this quote is "You can't take it with you!" Yet, as much as we hear this philosophy—and believe it—most of us accumulate things as if we were Pharaohs of Egypt, planning to cart our stuff with us into the next world.

To define true contentment, most people look to the past rather than the future. Long-married couples talk of when they had nothing but each other, yet discovered that was enough. Business leaders speak with passion of the early days when they worked out of the kitchen and shipped out of the garage. Contentment begins with little, but with the sense of purpose and a worthy struggle—an ideal not based on status or the clutter of material things.

We enter the world naked and gasping for breath; we leave it the same way. We carry nothing in or out. Whatever we have during our brief stay is ours only in the sense that we *manage* it for awhile. We never really own it.

Perhaps we need to loosen our grip on the things of this world and simplify our lives again. No amount of possessions can produce the contentment that comes from virtuous living in the presence of the Creator, who gave them all to us in the first place.

CONTENTED TO A FAULT

*To be content with even the best people, we must
be contented with little and bear a great deal.
Those who are most perfect have many
imperfections, and we have great faults.*

Fénelon

*I*t's the classic after-the-honeymoon scenario. The husband
discovers that his beautiful young wife isn't as chipper early in
the morning as she was during those late-night dates. The
bride begins to lose her husband's full attention during ball
games. And getting used to each other's bathroom routine—
well, that's a whole other story. Can they learn to live content-
edly ever after—in spite of their "many imperfections"?

Some couples do. Too many others don't. Some people are
willing to offer the time, patience, and love required to become
completely contented with someone else. But when people
ignore their own "great faults" and condemn others for lesser
ones, the results range from unpleasant to tragic—including
emotional withdrawal, divorce, abuse, and even suicide.

They say justice is blind, but mercy wears a blindfold as well.
A just judge must examine *all* the evidence. Yet for the sake of
contentment, we can *choose* to close our eyes to whatever might
prevent us from having to "bear a great deal."

Think about it: If you were more forgiving and less judgmen-
tal of others, how many additional "contented" friendships
might you have? Why don't you try it for a few weeks and find
out?

CONTENTMENT

Contentment is natural wealth,
luxury is artificial poverty.
Socrates

Godliness with contentment is great gain.
For we brought nothing into the world, and
we can take nothing out of it. But if we have
food and clothing, we will be content with that.
The Apostle Paul, New Testament

To be content with even the best people, we must
be contented with little and bear a great deal.
Those who are most perfect have many
imperfections, and we have great faults.
Fénelon

***C**ourage; N. the quality of mind or spirit that enables one to face difficulty, danger, pain, etc., with firmness and without fear; bravery; to act in accordance with one's beliefs, esp. in spite of criticism; fearlessness; fortitude; spirit; heroism; bravery; valor; courage permits one to face extreme dangers and difficulties without fear*

OUT OF THE BOX

Courage is rightly esteemed the first of human qualities,
because . . . it is the quality that guarantees all others.
Sir Winston Churchill

Suppose you buy a stereo with a money-back guarantee if it doesn't work. The next day you request a refund. The salesperson has some questions: Did you make the proper connections? Were the speakers attached properly? But then you explain that you never actually got around to taking it out of the box. You were just afraid that it wasn't going to work, so you didn't even try it out.

You would certainly get a strange look, whether or not you got your money back. The purpose of buying a new appliance is to rip it out of the box and see how that baby works! An appliance that remains in the box is only a doorstop.

Virtues are the same way. We may *think* we want these qualities in our lives, yet when the opportunity comes to "let them out of the box," sometimes we freeze up. We can't guarantee what will happen when these qualities begin to influence our relationships. Perhaps they will inconvenience us or result in personal sacrifices. That's why courage is so important. Without it, other virtues may remain "boxed in" indefinitely.

There are few guarantees in life, but you can be sure of one thing: If you know what virtues can do, but don't courageously put them into practice, you're likely to get double your disappointment in return.

CARELESS LIVING

*The paradox of courage is that a man must be a
little careless of his life even in order to keep it.*

G. K. Chesterton

*I*t may sound odd to recommend being careless of one's life,
yet Chesterton has a certain logic. If you're in a burning high-
rise and your only escape is to plunge into a minuscule net
being held by tiny firemen, your instinct may be to stay right
where you are. The fear of jumping can outweigh the need to
take action.

Fear is dangerous because it incapacitates us. We can cling
too tightly to certain aspects of life, just as we can the ledge of
a burning building. Fear prevents us from sharing possessions,
helping others, pursuing dreams, taking a minority stand even
when we're right, and much more. In such cases we need to be
a bit more "careless." Without the courage to take an occasional risk, we never discover how much better life can be.

Jesus once said, "The man who loves his life will lose it,
while the man who hates his life in this world will keep it for
eternal life" (John 12:25).

This tough paradox is not a command to be irresponsible or
foolish but a challenge to take the plunge into something or
Someone bigger than yourself. Do you have the courage to
accept the challenge?

COURAGE IN PROFILE

*Love of fame, fear of disgrace, schemes for
advancement, desire to make life comfortable and
pleasant, and the urge to humiliate others are often at
the root of the valour men hold in such high esteem.*
La Rochefoucauld

*I*n 1956 when John F. Kennedy wrote the Pulitzer prize winning *Profiles in Courage*, people almost always connected
courage with qualities such as duty, loyalty, and community.
But lately we've discovered that many "courageous" people
have ulterior motives. We've become cynical from seeing our
"heroes" exposed as greedy exploiters or self-centered opportunity seekers rather than being concerned for the good of
mankind.

You decide. What takes more courage?

- To live within your meager budget, or initiate a high-
  risk financial scam that pays off big if it works but
  lands you in jail if it doesn't

- To endure the empty insults of insignificant foreign
  leaders, or go to war in order to "humiliate" them

- To fight for your life and hope doctors learn something
  from your struggle against an intractable or terminal
  disease that will help others, or recruit a "death doctor" for a "comfortable and pleasant" death

The difference is motive. True courage is selfless; counterfeit
courage is selfish. If we find ourselves taking risks only for personal gain, we would be wise to reconsider our motives. When
you have genuine courage, you won't need the Wizard of Oz to
pin a medal to your chest. You'll know.

COURAGE

◆

---

*Courage is rightly esteemed the first of
human qualities, because . . . it is the
quality that guarantees all others.*
Sir Winston Churchill

*The paradox of courage is that a man must be a
little careless of his life even in order to keep it.*
G. K. Chesterton

*Love of fame, fear of disgrace, schemes for
advancement, desire to make life comfortable
and pleasant, and the urge to humiliate
others are often at the root of the valour
men hold in such high esteem.*
La Rochefoucauld

◆

***C**ourtesy; N. excellence of manners or social conduct; polite behavior; respectful or considerate act or expression; indulgence, consent, or acquiescence; favor, help, or generosity*
— Adj. gracious, courtly, civil

ON YOUR MARK . . .
GET SET . . . SMILE

Life is short, but there is always time for courtesy.
Ralph Waldo Emerson

*T*ry an experiment. Get a stopwatch or clock with a second hand and see how long it takes to do each of the following things:

- Smile
- Say "Please" or "Thanks"
- Wave in greeting to a neighbor
- Hold a door open for someone

You get the idea. These are things that require essentially no time—just the tiniest bit of effort. But what a difference they can make! A mere smile can lift the spirits of someone who has been having a bad day. Your "Thank you" may be the only expression of appreciation another person has heard in weeks. For the low investment you make in courtesy, the payoffs can be considerable.

How long does it take to go beyond mere manners: "You did a good job"; "You're looking nice today"; or "I appreciate your talents"? What does it hurt to let someone else take the closest parking spot or let someone in front of you at the supermarket checkout line or not to be the first one in when the doors open? It doesn't threaten your self-worth, but it does enhance others'.

Practicing courtesy won't make life any longer. But it will give other people more opportunities to look back with fondness and more reasons to move forward with hope. Isn't that worth a few seconds a day?

ARE YOU READY FOR THE TEST?

The test of good manners is to be able
to put up pleasantly with bad ones.
Wendall Willkie

*T*he virtue of courtesy might not seem as compelling as courage, honor, compassion, or love. Compared to other virtues, courtesy may be perceived as something of a no-brainer. If this is your thinking, you might want to reconsider.

Courtesy has a number of layers. At its most basic, it is equated with "niceness." You speak when spoken to, return thank-you notes for gifts, let the other person go first or have the larger half of the cookie. Nothing to it.

But at a deeper level, courtesy requires active humility, forgiveness, and self-control. At this level, courtesy becomes hard, tough, and disciplined. When someone insults you loudly and publicly, are you strong enough to offer a courteous reply? When a co-worker takes credit for your idea and makes you look like a lazy slacker, does courtesy go out the window? When a competitor uses every sneaky underhanded method to beat you out of a job, client, account, or the last piece of pie, can you remain calm, honest, and consistent?

You will face countless "tests" of courtesy in response to the bad manners of others. Like any other subject, in order to do well on hard tests you need to begin with the basics and keep learning as you go along. If you stay alert and know your subject, you'll do well on any pop quizzes that unexpectedly come your way.

EXCEPT FOR ONE THING

*A bad manner spoils everything, even reason and justice;
a good one supplies everything, gilds a NO, sweetens
truth, and adds a touch of beauty to old age itself.*
                                        Baltasar Grácian

*T*he world is filled with people who would be well-liked, have a lot of friends, and might even be famous if it weren't for one thing. That one thing varies from person to person. It might be an annoying laugh, body odor, a tendency to cling to others, a speech impediment, or any number of things. These people can be highly intelligent, funny, compassionate, and more. Yet that one thing prevents others from being comfortable around them.

In many cases the person has no control over his problem mannerism. But it's tragic when a person *willingly* displays an obnoxious personality that keeps his or her other assets so well hidden. No doubt you know people who are talented, brilliant, and have much to contribute—yet who practically dare people to like them. Their "bad manner" spoils anything positive they have to offer.

We should learn from these people and make sure we aren't doing the same thing. A self-check for bad mannerisms is in order. But we also need to take the initiative to get past the "one thing" that isolates so many people. Some of them will tell you where to go, but thousands more out there are desperate for a close friend.

Do you have a "good manner" strong enough to really care about these people? Or do you just think you do?

COURTESY

Life is short, but there is always time for courtesy.
Ralph Waldo Emerson

*The test of good manners is to be able
to put up pleasantly with bad ones.*
Wendall Willkie

*A bad manner spoils everything, even reason
and justice; a good one supplies everything,
gilds a NO, sweetens truth, and adds
a touch of beauty to old age itself.*
Baltasar Grácian

*D**iligence*; N. constant and earnest effort to accomplish what is undertaken; persistent exertion of body or mind; done or pursued with persevering attention; painstaking; industrious; tireless

DILIGENCE

EASY DOES IT

*What we hope to do with ease, we
must learn first to do with diligence.*
Samuel Johnson

"*I*t's like riding a bike. You never forget!"

How many times have you heard this phrase in regard to an acquired skill? Yet recall the diligence it took to learn to ride that bike in the first place: overcoming the fear of sitting so far above the ground, learning to control that wobbling front wheel, learning how to stop without wrecking.

Yet with diligent repetition the skill was eventually mastered and riding a bicycle became the simplest thing in the world. It was one of our first thrills of freedom. If only we would learn to be so diligent in other areas.

But in our world of sound bytes, half-hour sitcom plots, media blitzes, and everyone jostling to get his fifteen minutes of fame, it's rare to find anyone learning or practicing diligence. Students cheat or quit before applying themselves. Employees prefer equal (and certain) raises over rewards based on individual merit. Athletes demand multiyear contracts *before* they prove themselves.

Diligent people work hard for the sheer thrill of becoming better at what they do. They love the value of the task itself. Eventually success comes naturally to them. They make it look easy. Other people want to know their "secret." But there are no shortcuts to diligence. It's like riding a bike.

DILIGENCE RULES!

Diligent hands will rule, but laziness ends in slave labor.
King Solomon, Old Testament

*T*he story is told of a successful and prolific author who was approached by a young aspiring writer wanting to know his secret. The wise, established author had a simple reply: "Four pages a day."

Four pages doesn't sound like much. But four pages a day, *every* day, quickly accumulates. Such is the secret of diligence.

Some days it's easy to let our hands get lazy. But diligence requires *consistent* hard work, attention to the right priorities, and the ability to resist numerous temptations. Diligence gives us something to show for all our labor. Too often people work harder trying to *avoid* work than they would if they set their hands to the tasks that needed doing.

Laziness forces us to depend on others, which in time can lead to becoming enslaved to them. On the other hand, diligent hands allow us to take control of our lives and shape our own destinies.

What is your equivalent of "four pages a day"? Have you completed today's allotment? If not, why don't you put down this book and get to it? You don't want to have to do twice as much tomorrow.

DILIGENCE

○

*What we hope to do with ease, we
must learn first to do with diligence.*
Samuel Johnson

Diligent hands will rule, but laziness ends in slave labor.
King Solomon, Old Testament

○

*F*aith; N. confidence or trust in a person or thing; belief which is not based on proof; belief in God or in the doctrines or teachings of religion; a system of religious belief; the obligation of loyalty or fidelity to a person, promise, engagement; the observance of this obligation; fidelity to one's promise, oath, allegiance

OUT OF SIGHT, BUT STILL IN MIND

*A simple, childlike faith in a Divine Friend solves
all the problems that come to us by land or sea.*
Helen Keller

*T*he Bible tells us, "We live by faith, not by sight" (2 Corinthians 5:7). If so, Helen Keller must know something about faith. Put yourself in her place. How do you think you would cope in a life devoid of sight or sound? You would know *something* of an outside world, but it would certainly be a confusing one.

Many people would simply give up. But thanks to the devotion of teacher Anne Sullivan, Helen learned to communicate, to appreciate the world around her, and eventually to "see" beyond this world to the next. The faithfulness of a human friend led to Keller's faith in a "Divine Friend" for whom no problem was too big.

People today struggle to understand a spiritual world they cannot see with their eyes or hear with their ears, yet they sense it is "out there somewhere." They seek a Divine Friend, but they're looking for literal "sightings" rather than faith encounters.

The seekers of the world need dedicated helpers. And we *all* need childlike faith. As Helen Keller, let's find the faith to compensate for our lack of sight with a more important quality: *trust*. Then, when problems visit us, we'll have a Friend to depend on.

FAITH LIKE SOLID OAK

*Faith is an act of rational choice which determines us
to act as if certain things were true and in the
confident expectation that they will prove to be true.*
William R. Inge

What was your last act of faith?

Before you try to recall incidents of walking on water, moving mountains, or healing lepers, let's consider the Inge definition. Faith is not entirely a spiritual virtue. When you place a seed in the ground and expect it to grow, that is faith. Unless you are a botanist or have an excellent memory of high school biology, you don't fully understand how that huge oak tree comes from one little acorn, but you believe that it does.

When you make plans for tomorrow, you show faith that the sun will come up in the morning. When you entrust new privileges and responsibilities to your children, they see your faith in them to grow and mature. In this sense, everyone's life involves a considerable amount of faith. When you realize how much you are forced to "take on faith," even in the midst of scientific progress, the more sense it makes to put faith in Someone who is always consistent, dependable, and trustworthy.

The better we understand faith, the better we can choose *faithfulness*. Our goal should be to acquire the level of faith needed to make us more faithful in our dealings with others. Then others will be able to count on us as surely as the sun will rise tomorrow morning.

IMAGINE THAT

Use human means as though divine ones didn't exist,
and divine means as though there were no human ones.

Ignatius Loyola

*J*ohn Lennon offended many when he wrote "Imagine," with its "Imagine there's no heaven" premise. His point was that religion too often divides people instead of uniting them. Loyola makes a similar suggestion—but a more complete one that has a different purpose.

If we imagine there's no heaven, then anything good in the world is our responsibility. In one sense, that's a powerful and motivating thought. But to stop there (as Lennon did) is dangerous. We must also imagine the tremendous evil we're capable of when left to our own desires and devices. We can work as if there's no heaven, yet we require divine help for the wisdom, strength, and motivation to accomplish anything that is truly good.

When a sports team wins a play-off game, why does the coach get the credit? Didn't the *players* do the sweating, defending, and scoring? Sure they did, but the coach trained them, gave them the game plan, and inspired them to work together and win.

In matters of faith, we need to struggle just as hard as athletes in training. Yet we must also depend on our heavenly Coach. Besides, when the big game is over and it's "trophy time," the promise of heaven is tremendously comforting.

We can work as if everything is up to us. But imagine there's no heaven? Don't be ridiculous!

MINIMUM DEITY REQUIREMENTS

A little faith will bring your soul to heaven,
but a lot of faith will bring heaven to your soul.
Dwight L. Moody

*H*ave you ever noticed how many people want "just enough" religion in their lives—not so little that God would write them off, yet not so much that other people would think them strange? It must be hard to "walk the spiritual tightrope" an entire lifetime.

To Dwight L. Moody, faith was more than "fire insurance" that served as a ticket out of hell. He realized that genuine faith affected the quality of everyday living. Faith is a foundation for virtue because it helps us focus on the reason for our virtue and the One who rewards those who live the "good life."

Faith keeps us in touch with God—the source of power, perseverance, love, strength, and everything else good. Faith converts "religion" into "relationship." And as we build on that basic faith relationship with God, every other aspect of life is affected: words, actions, attitudes, interpersonal relationships, self-image. Faith is the filter that adds color to what previously seemed a bleak outlook on life. It brings a little patch of heaven to bland, earthly existence.

"Life Is Hell," an illustrated book series by Matt Groening, creator of "The Simpsons," is currently popular. But life doesn't have to be hell. When infused with more than a little faith, life can become quite heavenly.

FAITH

*A simple, childlike faith in a Divine Friend solves
all the problems that come to us by land or sea.*
Helen Keller

*Faith is an act of rational choice which determines us
to act as if certain things were true and in the
confident expectation that they will prove to be true.*
William R. Inge

*Use human means as though divine ones didn't exist,
and divine means as though there were no human ones.*
Ignatius Loyola

*A little faith will bring your soul to heaven,
but a lot of faith will bring heaven to your soul.*
Dwight L. Moody

*F**orgiveness*; N. act of forgiving;
disposition or willingness to forgive;
— V. to grant free pardon for or remission of
(an offense, debt, etc.): absolve; to give up
all claim on account of; remit (a debt, oblig-
ation, etc.); to grant free pardon to (a per-
son); to cease to feel resentment against;
absolve, acquit

ONE MORE TIME

Forgiveness is not an occasional act;
it is a permanent attitude.
Martin Luther King, Jr.

When asked if someone is a forgiving person, how do you determine your answer? You might conduct some objective research, interviewing everyone who ever came into contact with your subject and then compiling a case history. But, more than likely, you would draw on your own subjective knowledge—the most recent contact you had with the person. If he or she forgave your last offense, you would consider the person a forgiving one. If not, you wouldn't.

You might forgive someone for dozens of offenses. But all it takes is one instance of grudge-holding judgment to obliterate every act of forgiveness to date. When you think of your own relationships that have fallen apart, many can probably be traced to one thing that has been deemed "unforgivable." If you could only forgive that one thing, who knows where the relationship could go?

Martin Luther King, who sought to eradicate racial oppression, challenges us to a greater consistency of reconciliation. If we forgive only occasionally, we cannot consider ourselves forgiving people. As you learn to forgive "one more thing," and do so with greater consistency, forgiveness becomes a permanent attitude. And you'll appreciate the permanent difference it will make in your life.

PLAYING GOD

I think that if God forgives us we must forgive ourselves. Otherwise it is almost like setting up ourselves as a higher tribunal than Him.

C. S. Lewis

On a cruise you fall overboard, and you're not a good swimmer. Two things are tossed your direction. One is a life preserver attached by a sturdy rope to the ship. The other is a lead anchor on a heavy chain that will drag you to the bottom of the sea in a matter of seconds. Which do you grab?

It appears to be a simple choice. But make the situation a bit more symbolic, the life preserver symbolizing forgiveness and the anchor representing guilt. Would you give the same answer? Countless thousands of people are drowning in guilt because they simply will not forgive themselves.

Many people, even when they believe that God readily forgives them, continue to struggle with self-imposed guilt—sometimes for a lifetime. You hear comments such as "I wasn't a very good mother and now my kids have problems," or, "I was goofing off as a kid and gave someone a permanent disability." Usually when you hear of people "playing God," it refers to how they treat others. C. S. Lewis reminds us, however, that we can also play God in the area of self-condemnation.

If we insist on playing God, why focus on the past? Instead, why not work to bring healing in the present and provide peace and confidence in the future? Better yet, why not quit playing and trust that God knows what He's doing?

FORGIVENESS

◆

Forgiveness is not an occasional act;
it is a permanent attitude.
Martin Luther King, Jr.

I think that if God forgives us we must forgive
ourselves. Otherwise it is almost like setting
up ourselves as a higher tribunal than Him.
C. S. Lewis

◆

Friendship; N. a person attached to another by feelings of affection or personal regard; a person who gives assistance; a patron or supporter; one who is on good terms with another; one not hostile; ally, associate; friendly feeling or disposition; a friendly relation or intimacy

KISS AND TELL

Wounds from a friend can be trusted,
but an enemy multiplies kisses.
King Solomon, Old Testament

*P*eople say the truth hurts, yet one of the foremost responsibilities of genuine friends is to deal truthfully with each
other. So as much as friends might try to cushion truth with
love, sometimes they are wounded by each other's straight-
forwardness.

You can determine which option you prefer. If you want to
avoid painful truths, you can select the kind of "friend" who
always tells you what you want to hear ("who multiplies
kisses"). Such people aren't hard to find. Usually they want the
same treatment in return. But you'll always know, deep down,
that they don't have your best interests at heart. When people
are willing to skirt the truth in one area, they can never really
be trusted about anything else.

A true friend will tell you that a new boyfriend doesn't seem
right for you . . . that your new clothes appear to herald a
return to disco . . . that your treatment of someone seems too
harsh . . . that you need to quit certain harmful behaviors.
Such honest criticism can be quite painful and unwelcomed.

Yes, the truth may hurt. But sincere friends who regretfully
inflict wounds will still be there after the wounds heal. And
true friends, when wounded, will patiently endure the healing
process and won't keep track of the scars.

THE BEST OF FRIENDS

*By friendship you mean the greatest love, the
greatest usefulness, the most open communication,
the noblest sufferings, the severest truth, the
heartiest counsel, and the greatest union of minds
of which brave men and women are capable.*

Jeremy Taylor

"*L*et's be friends." This phrase has a lot of different meanings. For young children on a playground, it can be an invitation to simple companionship; between adolescents, perhaps a prelude to romance; between people who haven't gotten along in the past, an invitation for reconciliation. But these are just beginnings. We rarely think in terms of the depth of commitment described by Jeremy Taylor.

No one develops a deep, abiding relationship without intentionally investing time, honesty, vulnerability, and ever-increasing levels of love. Think about your friendships in light of Taylor's statement:

- In what ways do you express love in your friendships?
- How are your friendships "useful"?
- In what special ways do you relate to friends?
- What sufferings have you endured together?
- What truths have you discovered from each other?
- What helpful counsel have you received from others?
- What stories can you tell about your "union of minds"?

Perhaps the most important word in the quote is "brave." If you have many acquaintances but few close relationships, take the plunge. Explore the depths of life together as friends.

FITTING IN

*In the progress of personality, first comes a declaration
of independence, then a recognition of interdependence.*
Henry van Dyke

*H*ave you ever found yourself involved in a friendship where
the other person was *too* eager to be your friend? Five minutes
after meeting him, it becomes difficult to do anything on your
own or with other friends without him standing in your
shadow. Sound familiar?

We *all* enter the world depending on others, but some children never outgrow dependence on their parents. Others trans-
fer their dependence to a continuing sequence of "friends."
They suck the life from one person and then move on to someone else like a thirsty mosquito.

Until a person becomes independent, he simply can't be a
very good friend because he has nothing to contribute to the
relationship. All he can do is take. Only people who indepen-
dently discover and develop their own unique personalities are
able to interact with others.

A jigsaw puzzle may have thousands of pieces of all shapes
and colors. But when properly assembled, the finished product
is much more impressive than any single piece. Such are
friendships. Only by maintaining our unique shapes, colors,
and personalities will we be able to discover "the big picture."

If you haven't yet declared your independence, isn't it time to
sign your John Hancock on the dotted line? And if you're independent but not yet interdependent, won't you find the place
where you fit? There still seem to be several missing pieces.

FRIENDSHIP RIPENS SLOWLY

To the Ancients, Friendship seemed the happiest and most fully human of all loves; the crown of life and the school of virtue. The modern world, in comparison, ignores it.

C. S. Lewis

When C. S. Lewis wrote *The Four Loves*, he divided love into affection, erotic love, divine love, and friendship. He suggests a drastic decline in the priority people once placed on friendship. It's not that people don't *want* to be friends. Few experiences in life are as rewarding as spending an evening with friends whom we know intimately. So perhaps the problem has to do with time.

Of the four loves, friendship can be the most time consuming. We have to be available, become vulnerable, share our interests, accept and know people for what they are, learn to listen. Friendship requires above-average giving of oneself.

In the "modern" world, many of us are not willing to commit to the time required to share more and more of ourselves with more and more people. We start by limiting the *number* of our friendships. Then we limit the level of our *openness*. Sure enough, we create more time to do other things, but we sacrifice a lot as well. Perhaps the problem is really selfishness. Yet self-enhancement occurs when the virtues of friends, as Lewis suggests, rub off on us.

The privilege of making and strengthening friendships is like possessing the goose that lays golden eggs. Each friendship is of great value. But when we get impatient with the process, we're in danger of losing everything.

FRIENDSHIP

---

*Wounds from a friend can be trusted,
but an enemy multiplies kisses.*
King Solomon, Old Testament

*By friendship you mean the greatest love, the greatest
usefulness, the most open communication, the
noblest sufferings, the severest truth, the heartiest
counsel, and the greatest union of minds
of which brave men and women are capable.*
Jeremy Taylor

*In the progress of personality, first comes a declaration
of independence, then a recognition of interdependence.*
Henry van Dyke

*To the Ancients, Friendship seemed the happiest and most
fully human of all loves; the crown of life and the school
of virtue. The modern world, in comparison, ignores it.*
C. S. Lewis

*F**rugality**; Adj. economical in use or expenditure; prudently saving or sparing; entailing little expense; economical; self-denying, thrifty; provident, careful*

HARD WORK OR FAST CASH?

The way to wealth is as plain as the way to market. It depends chiefly on two words, industry and frugality; that is, waste neither time nor money, but make the best of both.
Benjamin Franklin

*I*n 1986 a man won $7.5 million in a state lottery. In 1992 he was arrested for burning down his expensive new home. He said his life had become "a living hell" because of so many people requesting money from him, and he just "snapped."

There are two sure paths to frustration. The first is to work hard all your life and never have anything to show for it. The second is to receive an unearned fortune from an outside source and get the reputation for having everything handed to you. Of the two problems, most of us would prefer the second, but both are frustrating.

Ben Franklin had the answer. First, we should work hard. Time is a commodity that, like money, can be budgeted, invested, or squandered. When time is put to good use in profitable work, we make a living and feel good about ourselves. But it's easy to "reward" ourselves by spending *everything* we earn.

So frugality, the second step, complements hard work. We save and watch our earnings accumulate. The slow and steady results of frugality aren't as thrilling as winning the lottery, but the odds of truly "winning" in the long run are a whole lot better.

FRUGALITY

A QUAKER STATE OF MIND

Frugality is good, if liberality be joined with it.
The first is leaving off superfluous expenses; the last
bestowing them to the benefit of others that need.
William Penn

*W*hen you think of Quakers, what's the first thing that comes to mind? Black hats? Old-fashioned values? Good cooking? A simplified lifestyle? Oatmeal? One thing that doesn't leap to mind is "big spenders."

William Penn puts frugality into perspective for us. We should be careful and accountable with our money. That doesn't mean, however, that we should scrimp and deny ourselves to the extreme—only to die bitter and alone, leaving behind a huge fortune for a house full of cats.

No. The purpose of making do with a little less is to help someone else who could use a little more. Frugality without purpose creates misers. But frugality with others in mind is a tremendous challenge—and privilege. In many cases it creates a chain of gratitude that originates from you . . . to the person helped . . . to many others.

This is one of those quotes that, for many of us, "sounds good in theory," but until you actually practice frugality and see how your personal sacrifice affects someone else, the theory is untested. So do it because, as another "Quaker" spokesperson (Wilford Brimley) says, "It's the right thing to do."

FRUGALITY

---

*The way to wealth is as plain as the way
to market. It depends chiefly on two words,
industry and frugality; that is, waste neither
time nor money, but make the best of both.*
Benjamin Franklin

*Frugality is good, if liberality be joined with it.
The first is leaving off superfluous expenses; the last
bestowing them to the benefit of others that need.*
William Penn

Generosity; N. readiness or liberality in giving; freedom from meanness or smallness of mind or character; largeness or fullness; amplitude; bountifulness; nobleness; magnanimity; fertile; prolific; open-handed, free; plentiful, copious; fruitful

GENEROSITY ON LAYAWAY

If you are not generous with a meager income,
you will never be generous with abundance.

Harold Nye

A classic rock song proclaims, "I'll sleep when I'm dead." The song proposes squeezing just as much out of life while you can—and dealing with the consequences later on.

Similarly, the "live now, pay later" philosophy affects generosity. One widespread attitude is "I'll give when I'm rich." How many times have you heard people proclaim—or even pray—"If I won the lottery, I would give my church a million dollars"? Yet if all those people would put their money into the collection plate each week instead of spending it on lottery tickets, the church would come out far ahead.

A change in income does not initiate a change in habits. More money does not make people more generous. In fact, it usually has the opposite result: If we are protective of a little bit of money, we become more protective with larger amounts. When it comes to generosity, the teaching of Jesus almost always holds true: "Give, and it will be given to you. A good measure, pressed down, shaken together and running over, will be poured into your lap. For with the measure you use, it will be measured to you" (Luke 6:38).

Either you are a generous person from the start, or you aren't. The determining factor is not your bank balance but your heart. It's easier to have a change of heart if you learn the joy of giving.

GETTING (AND GIVING) A LIFE

We make a living by what we get,
but we make a life by what we give.
Sir Winston Churchill

*I*f someone asked "What do you do to make a living?" you would probably have a ready answer. But if you were asked "What are you doing to make a life?" you might find the question puzzling.

Generosity may be the virtue that best differentiates "making a living" from "making a life." Don't be fooled into thinking that generosity is simply giving money to other people. Generosity need not have anything to do with money. You can

- Invite a struggling college student to have a meal with your family.
- Stay with a friend's kids so he or she can have some solitude.
- Do grocery shopping for (then visiting with) someone who is shut in.
- Double your brownie recipe so you'll have a batch to give away.
- Do more than your fair share of a big team project at work.

None of these things are very expensive or time consuming. So many actions of generous people seem insignificant to them, yet mean much more to the recipient(s). Think about this for a while. Then the next time you hear the trendy expression "Get a life!" you can say you gave yours away.

GENEROSITY SOUNDS FISHY

A man there was, though some did count him mad.
The more he cast away, the more he had.

John Bunyan

*A*s John Bunyan sat in prison, he was a poor man who didn't have much left to "cast away." But he had his own story to offer, and it became the allegorical classic *Pilgrim's Progress*. For many years it was the best-selling book, next to the Bible.

When we see people who give things away rather than hoarding them, we're usually quick to "count the person mad." And if it's *temporary* insanity, we may be among the crowd trying to collect. But generosity is the *habit* of casting away—not indiscriminately, but toward a specific purpose.

Think of a fisherman. He or she may spend entire days "casting away," and, the more time spent in casting, the better the haul of fish at the end of the day. The benefits of casting away personal assets is not so tangible, but the same principles apply. Anyone can give up things of no value—possessions that are outgrown, outmoded, and outdated. That's not generosity. True generosity is giving to meet someone else's need, even if it requires personal sacrifice. The action may appear "mad" to others, but the benefits include satisfaction, joy, and empathy.

Try it for yourself and see. Start casting away like a fisherman and see what you "catch." But remember, when it comes to generosity, there are no strings attached.

GIVE AND GET IT OVER WITH

The proper aim of giving is to put the recipient in a state where he no longer needs our gift.
C. S. Lewis

What motivates you to give to a worthwhile cause? Many of us funnel our gifts through large charitable organizations. They aggressively solicit our help, so we return a check in their prepaid envelope, phone in a pledge during their telethon, or drop a few dollars in their bucket while stopped at a light. It's easy and tax deductible. The trade-off is that we rarely see the results of our giving. And the need still seems endless.

There's another kind of giving: giving toward specific, individual needs—perhaps needs that few other people know about. Such gifts help people get back on their feet. And when we see the good it does, *we* benefit as well as the recipients. We start giving, see the need eliminated, and start over again elsewhere.

Giving becomes exciting. It no longer depends on an endless barrage of solicitations but becomes instead an endless opportunity to meet real and present *seen* needs. Sometimes it's money, sometimes advice or time. But it always contributes to the other person's self-sufficiency rather than continued dependence.

The tax advantages of such giving are not always as significant, but other benefits are usually far greater.

GENEROSITY

If you are not generous with a meager income,
you will never be generous with abundance.
Harold Nye

We make a living by what we get,
but we make a life by what we give.
Sir Winston Churchill

A man there was, though some did count him mad.
The more he cast away, the more he had.
John Bunyan

The proper aim of giving is to put the recipient
in a state where he no longer needs our gift.
C. S. Lewis

***G**entleness; Adj. kindly, amiable; mild; not severe, rough, or violent; moderate; gradual; of good birth or family; characteristic of good birth; honorable; respectable; easily handled or managed; tractable; soft or low; polite; refined; noble; chivalrous*

GENTLE GIANTS

Nothing is so strong as gentleness,
and nothing so gentle as real strength.
Ralph Stockman

*P*erhaps you remember "Gentle Ben," the TV show whose title character was an enormous bear who wouldn't hurt anyone under any circumstances. Maybe you watched "Kung Fu," wherein Caine had the knowledge and agility to kick sense into anyone—yet preferred a gentle approach to life's conflicts. Even King Kong had a gentle side, as seen in his treatment of Fay Wray while climbing the Empire State Building.

But times have changed. Combining strength with *gentleness* seems to have disappeared as a TV plot as well as a lifestyle goal. The two qualities are still a marketable combination for, say, a laundry detergent. But where people are concerned, these are the days of "trash talk" on the ball courts and in-your-face victory dances in the end zone.

When was the last time you recall someone "turning the other cheek" when offended, or voluntarily going "the second mile" after being forced to endure the first one? That kind of gentle response is indeed rare.

Bears and big monkeys can be taught that true strength must be controlled. But what we need more is human beings with the character of impressive strength expressed gently.

WINNING BY A HAIR

Use a sweet tongue, courtesy, and gentleness, and thou mayest manage to guide an elephant by a hair.
Sa'di Gulistan

*Y*ou can't really appreciate this quote until you get in mind some of the "elephants" in your life that need guiding. Elephants are large and threatening. There's always a possibility that a "rogue elephant" will break loose and trample everything in its path. So what would you say are *your* current elephants? A rebellious child? A boss with a bad temper? A friend or relative with a major problem?

When you get someone in mind, try to imagine guiding that elephant by a hair. It would seem that, when dealing with an elephant, it would be much safer to stand behind and try to drive it. But that's not how gentleness works.

It takes courage to be gentle. It means you stand in front to lead and guide. You provide direction and offer support, verbal affirmation, and complete respect for the massive bulk behind you. If you put too much pressure on the hair you're tugging, you'll rip it out and perhaps annoy the elephant. You can't fake gentleness. It takes determination, concentration, and patience.

It's much safer for *you* to stand behind and make a lot of noise in an attempt to motivate your elephants. But the danger remains for them—and others in their path. So stand in front, be charming and courteous, and become the gentle leader you're capable of being. Then you'll need only a slim hair rather than a stout, menacing club.

GENTLENESS

Nothing is so strong as gentleness,
and nothing so gentle as real strength.
Ralph Stockman

Use a sweet tongue, courtesy, and gentleness, and
thou mayest manage to guide an elephant by a hair.
Sa'di Gulistan

***G**oodness; N. moral excellence; virtue; kindly feeling; kindness; generosity; excellence of quality; the best part of anything; a euphemism for God; right; proper; honorable or worthy; educated and refined; genuine; dependable; responsible*

GOOD AND PLENTY

Do all the good you can, in all the ways you can, to all the souls you can, in every place you can, at all the times you can, with all the zeal you can, as long as ever you can.
John Wesley

*D*o you think Wesley thought goodness was important? It's as if he is responding to a newspaper reporter's questions. Consequently, he provides an excellent outline for us to use:

What? "All the good you can"—In your normal daily routine, what opportunities do you have to do good things?

How? "In all the ways you can . . . with all the zeal you can"—After you know *what* to do, consider *how* to address the opportunities. How can you add *zeal* to your efforts?

Who? "To all the souls you can"—What names come to mind who could benefit from a good deed on your part?

Where? "In every place you can"—Recall every place you went last week. Where do you plan to go *this* week that could benefit from a good deed?

When? "At all the times you can"—enough said.

Why? Because that's why we are on this planet, and time is running out.

We don't determine the "as long as ever you can" part. We might have decades; we might have seconds. So we need to act *now.* Someday *we* may be in need of a good turn, and it will be too bad if we haven't shown others how it's done.

THE APPLE DOESN'T FALL FAR FROM THE TREE

Every good tree bears good fruit, but a bad tree bears bad fruit. . . . By their fruit you will recognize them.
Jesus Christ, New Testament

*I*s anything much more disappointing than buying exquisite looking apples only to discover at home that the cardboard packaging has more flavor? Sometimes we think we've discovered good fruit only to be severely disappointed when we discover the truth.

The same is true of people. Some dress themselves up, speak with silver-tongued ease, and pass themselves off as the nicest people you'd ever want to meet. But if they are up to no good, they will be found out eventually. Similarly, a good person might have a somewhat brash, crude, or otherwise suspicious exterior. Yet he or she always seems to come through during times of need.

Goodness, or lack of it, drives a person's actions. Nothing can keep goodness hidden for long if it's there—or pass for goodness if it's absent. A person's true nature is like an aroma—the closer you get, the better you can determine whether it's pleasant or obnoxious.

If an outsider witnessed *your* "fruit" (actions) of the past several weeks and knew nothing else about you, would he or she define you as "good"? If the answer doesn't agree with the assumptions you're making about yourself, you have some work to do.

THIS LITTLE LIGHT OF MINE

How far that little candle throws his beams!
So shines a good deed in a naughty world.
William Shakespeare

*T*hey entered a cave with a variety of good flashlights, but still had much difficulty winding through the narrow passageway—stumbling and running into each other, with their lights in every direction. On the way out they put away their flashlights and each carried only one lit candle instead. The difference was amazing. The candles provided more than enough light to make the return journey pleasant and trouble-free.

Much of life's focus is like a flashlight beam—high-intensity, and targeted on one small area: self-centered goals, carefully chosen friends, limited relationships. But the few acts of goodness we do are more like candles, spreading light equally in all directions (including back toward ourselves).

If the world was "naughty" in Shakespeare's time, today it is worse—vile, evil, perverse. We are more in need of "good deeds" than ever before. People of virtue must demonstrate goodness in order to blast away the surrounding darkness. The more light we can generate, the farther the darkness must retreat.

Perhaps you want the world to be a better place. It is said that it's better to light a candle than curse the darkness. Isn't it worth a try—for goodness' sake?

ROCKY ROAD

*Anyone who proposes to do good must not expect
people to roll stones out of his way, but must accept
his lot calmly if they even roll a few more upon it.*

Albert Schweitzer

*M*ost of us want to be thought of as a "good person." But we
define good by our own personal standards and are reluctant
to admit that some people might be better. To us, those people
become "goody two-shoes" or some other disparaging name.

You can probably recall school days and how "normal" students felt about someone trying to be *too* good. The goody-
goody person was ridiculed. Verbal stones were not only rolled
into his path but were hurled at him with full force.

Later in our life, the "too good" people are just as baffling.
Those who forsake profit-making ventures to join the Peace
Corps, become missionaries (like Schweitzer), work with the
homeless, or pursue other worthwhile goals make us feel a bit
guilty. And rather than admitting the guilt, we callously
assume, "There must be something wrong with that person. He
or she must not be able to make it in the 'real world.'" We are
quick to roll out the stones.

You would think that people devoted to goodness would have
a smooth path. But such is not the case. Schweitzer points out
that such people will "accept their lot calmly." You might not
be able to jog with ease down the road of goodness, but, then,
with the right attitude, rock climbing can be just as enjoyable.

GOODNESS

Do all the good you can, in all the ways you can, to all the souls you can, in every place you can, at all the times you can, with all the zeal you can, as long as ever you can.
John Wesley

Every good tree bears good fruit, but a bad tree bears bad fruit. . . . By their fruit you will recognize them.
Jesus Christ, New Testament

*How far that little candle throws his beams!
So shines a good deed in a naughty world.*
William Shakespeare

Anyone who proposes to do good must not expect people to roll stones out of his way, but must accept his lot calmly if they even roll a few more upon it.
Albert Schweitzer

Gratitude; N. the quality or feeling of being grateful or thankful; — Adj. warmly or deeply appreciative of kindness or benefits received; thankful; pleasing to the mind or senses; agreeable or welcome; refreshing; obliged, indebted; a warm or deep appreciation of personal kindness as shown to one; giving thanks, as to a benefactor or to a merciful Providence

PILGRIMS' DIGRESS

*In noble hearts the feeling of gratitude
has all the ardor of a passion.*
Poincelot

*H*appy Thanksgiving!

What? You say it's not Thanksgiving day? Well, it should be. One of the problems with gratitude is that we've designated only one day a year to be thankful. And what do we do on that single day that we set aside? Cook. Prepare for company. Watch football. Reunite as families only to renew old conflicts. Overeat. And maybe—just maybe—someone hurriedly says "grace" before the herd chows down.

We seem to have lost the willingness or ability to show gratitude for what we have. It is not a *passion;* it isn't even a priority. What we should take with gratitude we take for granted.

The Pilgrims would grieve to see what Thanksgiving has become. They had so many reasons to be thankful: being alive after a hazardous journey across the ocean; freedom from those who previously oppressed them; new friends and a new home. And while food wasn't *always* abundant, it was at this particular time.

Life. Freedom. Friends. Food and other necessities. These are all gifts from God. If we can't be passionately grateful for them, what have we become?

No, today might not be Thanksgiving Day. But tomorrow can be. The pilgrims had a bright vision of a new community based on virtue. They began with gratitude. So can you.

GREATER GRATEFULNESS

We can be thankful to a friend for a few acres
or a little money; and yet . . . for the great benefits
of our being, our life, health, and reason,
we look upon ourselves as under no obligation.

Seneca

*T*hink about the possessions you consider "treasures." What makes them so special? In many cases, perhaps the thing itself is less significant than the giver. Your treasures might include a wedding ring, an inheritance from a loved one, a handmade article, or even original works of art attached to your refrigerator by magnets.

Occasionally we express gratitude for our treasures, but rarely to the same extent that we complain about what we *don't* have. Likewise, a healthy person may never think twice about good health. But let him come down with forty-eight-hour stomach flu and everyone is likely to hear about it for weeks.

As Seneca points out, our possessions are small change compared to things of genuine value: health, mental stability, and life itself. If we are reluctant to thank peers, how can we "oblige" ourselves to a greater unseen Giver? If we take for granted the major gifts in life, how much genuine gratitude can we show for lesser things?

Once you stop taking so much for granted and make an initial commitment to a greater level of gratitude, it's surprising how quickly you'll discover how blessed you really are.

GRATITUDE

◆

*In noble hearts the feeling of gratitude
has all the ardor of a passion.*

Poincelot

*We can be thankful to a friend for a few acres
or a little money; and yet . . . for the great benefits
of our being, our life, health, and reason,
we look upon ourselves as under no obligation.*

Seneca

◆

H*onesty; N. sincerity or frankness; freedom from deceit or fraud; justice; veracity;*
— Adj. honorable in principles, intentions, and actions; upright; an honest person; showing fairly; sincere; frank; genuine or unadulterated; respectable; having a good reputation; truthful or creditable; humble, plain, or unadorned; just; trustworthy; straightforward, candid; pure

VERY TRULY YOURS

I hope I shall possess firmness and virtue enough
to maintain what I consider the most enviable
of all titles, the character of an honest man.

George Washington

*H*e was known as General, Commander-in-Chief, President, Father of his country. All of these are coveted titles. Yet the title deemed "most enviable" by George Washington was "honest."

How many of us can say the same? When given the choice between a bigger and better title by being ever-so-slightly dishonest or holding steadfast to the virtue of honesty, which do we choose? We like to think we're honest people. Yet when the tempting title of Graduate, Supervisor, CEO, Senator, or whatever, is dangled before us, it's amazing how many forms of dishonesty we're capable of.

We tell "little white lies" about competitors. We tell only part of the story, omitting what doesn't make us look good. We cheat—just enough to stay on top. We take credit for the work of other people. We use flattery to people's faces and then slander them behind their backs. We call it salesmanship, creative license, exaggeration, personal opinion—but it all boils down to dishonesty.

George Washington makes two important points:

- Honesty is a foundational virtue. If we don't hold it in the highest esteem, it will quickly escape us.

- Honesty requires *firmness*. The inner intention must be backed by a determined commitment.

It's worth pursuing. After all, would George Washington tell a lie?

AN HONEST MISTAKE

There is no well-defined boundary line between
honesty and dishonesty. The frontiers of
one blend with the outside limits of the other.
O. Henry

*T*oday we're having a pop quiz. Please answer honestly.

TRUE   FALSE

☐   ☐   1. I'm a better person than many people I know.

☐   ☐   2. My family is really messed up.

☐   ☐   3. If my friends took my advice, they would be much better off.

☐   ☐   4. God is unfair to make me suffer when selfish people have money and good lives.

☐   ☐   5. Whoever wrote this quiz must have severe psychological problems.

Perhaps the "frontiers" of honesty and dishonesty blend so readily because honesty doesn't necessarily have anything to do with truth. You can express honest opinions, yet be 100 percent wrong. Since the quiz statements are opinion-based, you can honestly believe that the writer has psychological problems, yet that doesn't necessarily mean it's true that he does. You can think God is unfair; that doesn't mean He is.

While honesty is indeed a virtue, it cannot stand alone. It needs the companion virtues of truth, gentleness, and especially love. You can be honest without being truthful. You can speak the truth without being honest. But you cannot express love without basing it on truth *and* honesty. When we get our priorities straight, the boundaries between honesty and dishonesty usually clear up pretty quickly.

THE BEST POLICY?

*Honesty is for the most part less
profitable than dishonesty.*

Plato

*I*t doesn't take a big-name philosopher like Plato to figure out
that dishonesty pays better than honesty. When a kid finds and
returns a wallet with $1,000 in it—only to receive a measly $5
reward from the tightwad owner—he learns the lesson. When a
student sees her peers make A's for cheating when she gets a C+
after weeks of research and hard work, another lesson is
learned. As kids grow up, they see the truth of this lesson in
hundreds of additional ways.

We all must decide whether to pursue an apparently prof-
itable course of dishonesty or to cling tenaciously to honesty.
The question becomes, "Why be honest if it isn't profitable?"
Your answer depends on your definition of "profitable."

In business a *monetary* profit is necessary or the business
folds. But is the same criterion true for a person's life? If your
"bottom line" has a dollar sign, you'll probably agree with
Plato's statement. But many people believe that "virtue is its
own reward" and takes precedence over financial gain. Self-
worth is more important than net worth. Honesty, therefore, is
more profitable than cash. So is generosity, frugality, and all
the other virtues.

They tell you honesty is the best policy. But they usually let
you find out for yourself that you'll never get rich from it.

HONESTY

*I hope I shall possess firmness and virtue enough
to maintain what I consider the most enviable
of all titles, the character of an honest man.*
George Washington

*There is no well-defined boundary line between
honesty and dishonesty. The frontiers of one
blend with the outside limits of the other.*
O. Henry

*Honesty is for the most part less
profitable than dishonesty.*
Plato

*H**onor*; N. high public esteem; fame; glory; honesty or integrity in one's beliefs and actions; a source of credit or distinction; high respect, as for worth, merit, or rank; the privilege of being associated with or receiving a favor from a respected person; uprightness

ABOVE AND BEYOND

*He has honor if he holds himself to an ideal
of conduct though it is inconvenient,
unprofitable, or dangerous to do so.*
Walter Lippman

*O*ne of the most coveted awards in the United States is the Congressional Medal of Honor, granted by Congress to a member of the armed forces for gallantry and bravery in combat, at the risk of life above and beyond the call of duty. Honor is one of those things that's hard to define, but you know it (and can reward it) when you see it.

What would motivate you to do something that is inconvenient? What would convince you to do something you wouldn't profit from? What would it take for you to willingly do something dangerous? These are things we normally try to avoid at all costs. But honor is an extraordinary attribute. At times the convenient thing, the profitable thing, and the safe thing is simply not the right thing to do. A sense of honor may be the only thing that keeps us on the course we know to be the correct one.

Unless you are, or have been, on a battlefield, no matter how honorable you are, you will never receive the Congressional Medal of Honor to hang around your neck. Nevertheless, others will benefit from your commitment. And the inner awareness that you are a person of honor makes the difficult choices easier. That should be reward enough.

MAY I ADDRESS YOUR HONOR?

Not everything which the law allows is honorable.
Legal maxim

*I*f you sit down and read through any code of law—from the opening books of the Old Testament to the latest laws of your community—you will see the intent of the creators of those laws. The *spirit* of the law is almost always clear. Yet no matter how well-written the codes, times change quickly and circumstances vary. Soon people who look only at the *letter* of the law can find "loopholes" and "cracks in the system." And if such people are devious, they can take advantage of others without risk of retribution because of some legal glitch.

That's why honor is so important. Sometimes being a "law-abiding citizen" is not enough. If we start with law, honor isn't necessarily a by-product. But if we start with a commitment to honor, we usually have no problem doing what the law details.

Adherence to the law is external. It's what other people see. Honor is the unseen internal quality that motivates us to do what is right, no matter what is (or isn't) written on the legal books. Honor also allows us to do *more* than what is required by law.

There are no loopholes when it comes to honor. If you even start to look for them, that's a sign that honor is a virtue you still need to work on.

HONOR AMONG COWARDS

It is the nature of the many to be amenable
to fear but not to the sense of honor.

Aristotle

*H*uman nature is often hard to fathom, yet Aristotle seems to have a clear flash of insight. Many people appear to have a sense of honor. Think of personal acquaintances you would place in this category. Then consider if any of them might do one of the following *if they were absolutely sure they would not be found out:*

- Slightly falsify a tax return to get a heftier return
- Exact quiet revenge on a spiteful enemy who has insulted them in some way
- Tell a little lie to avoid jury duty
- Spread unsubstantiated gossip, even under the guise of helping the person
- Cheat (just a little) in order to get a much-needed grant or promotion

Many times honor is something determined externally. From childhood, when parents told us to do things "or else," we have let fear of punishment motivate behavior. Some of us never outgrow a motivation based on possible negative consequences. We're afraid of what authority figures will do to us, so we behave ourselves.

But until honor is internalized, we can't lay claim to it. So how about *you*? Do you behave because it's right and part of your character? Or are you just scared?

HONOR

◆

*He has honor if he holds himself to an ideal
of conduct though it is inconvenient,
unprofitable, or dangerous to do so.*
Walter Lippman

Not everything which the law allows is honorable.
Legal maxim

*It is the nature of the many to be amenable
to fear but not to the sense of honor.*
Aristotle

◆

*H**ope*; N. the feeling that what is desired is also possible, or that events may turn out for the best; grounds for this feeling in a particular instance; a person in whom or thing in which expectations are centered; to place trust; expectancy; longing

FAITH'S FAITHFUL SIDEKICK

As wisdom without courage is futile, even so faith
without hope is nothing worth; for hope
endures and overcomes misfortune and evil.
Martin Luther

*W*hat would you think about a military leader who had a masterful plan to win a major battle with little loss among his own troops, yet was scared to implement it and therefore caused his men continued suffering? You probably would not have much respect for him. But what if *you* had a wise plan to improve your life with a new job, a big move, or some other tactic, yet were too scared to implement it and therefore caused yourself and those around you continued suffering?

We're usually pretty hard on other people when we see "wisdom without courage," yet we always have a good excuse when the same problem affects our own lives. Since other portions of this book deal with courage, let's keep the focus here on *hope*.

Just as we like to think we're wise, yet are scared, we may also consider ourselves faithful even while acting hopeless. But Webster defines hope as "desire accompanied by expectation of or belief in fulfillment." By this definition, faith and hope are not very different. It is this kind of enduring and expectant hope that allows us to "overcome misfortune and evil."

Hope as a "last resort" is essentially worthless. But hope as an anchor gets us through a lot of storms we will face in life. We need the courage to act on our wisdom. And we need the kind of hope that makes faith come alive and flourish.

BEYOND HOPE

Work without hope draws nectar in a sieve,
And hope without an object cannot live.
Samuel Taylor Coleridge

*T*his Coleridge quote parallels a familiar one by Henry David Thoreau: "The mass of men lead lives of quiet desperation." Hope is a much-needed antidote for desperation. Without hope, the joys and pleasures of life (the "nectar") turn sour or escape altogether.

Yet hope is useless unless it is hope in *something or someone.* Hope must have an object. When Penelope Pureheart is tied to the railroad tracks by the evil villain, her hope is in Dudley Dooright to come to the rescue. When the soldiers in the remote fort are out of supplies and surrounded by hostile renegades, their hope is in the approaching cavalry. So when your serenity is threatened by meaninglessness at work or a personal tragedy, in what do you place *your* hope?

As Coleridge suggests, our work occasionally creates situations in which we need hope. If the object of our hope is money, self-sufficiency, or power, we have doubtless been disappointed time and time again. But if the object of our hope is Someone who is more powerful and trustworthy than any problem we will ever face, then hope has a solid object indeed.

Remember that beyond hope is its object. So if you think that *you're* beyond hope, perhaps you're only moving beyond yourself and closer to Him.

BE A HOPE-TIMIST

*Hope means expectancy when
things are otherwise hopeless.*
G. K. Chesterton

*I*t is said that an optimist is a poor man who orders an expensive seafood platter in a fancy restaurant, planning to pay for it with the pearl he expects to find in his oyster. In contrast, pessimists are people who do not shake hands when they meet; they shake their heads instead.

Perhaps the primary difference between optimists and pessimists is hope—which Chesterton defines as expectancy. It's naive to expect a pearl in every oyster, a big lottery win exactly when money is needed, or a problem-free life. Yet to completely do away with a sense of hopeful expectancy is to condemn oneself to life with a dark outlook.

Much of what we experience is self-fulfilling prophecy. You might go to what you feel is a "hopeless" family reunion thinking, *These things are never any fun. We're going to get on each other's nerves and call each other a bunch of awful names.* If so, that's probably exactly what will happen. But hope allows you to tell yourself, *These things have been a pain in the past, but I'm going to do everything within my power to see that this one is better.*

Pessimists who don't try to make things better never do. Optimists who look on the bright side don't always make things better either. But they do *sometimes.* When that happens, they see the value of "expectancy when things are otherwise hopeless." And that's enough.

HOPE

As wisdom without courage is futile, even so faith without hope is nothing worth; for hope endures and overcomes misfortune and evil.
Martin Luther

Work without hope draws nectar in a sieve, And hope without an object cannot live.
Samuel Taylor Coleridge

Hope means expectancy when things are otherwise hopeless.
G. K. Chesterton

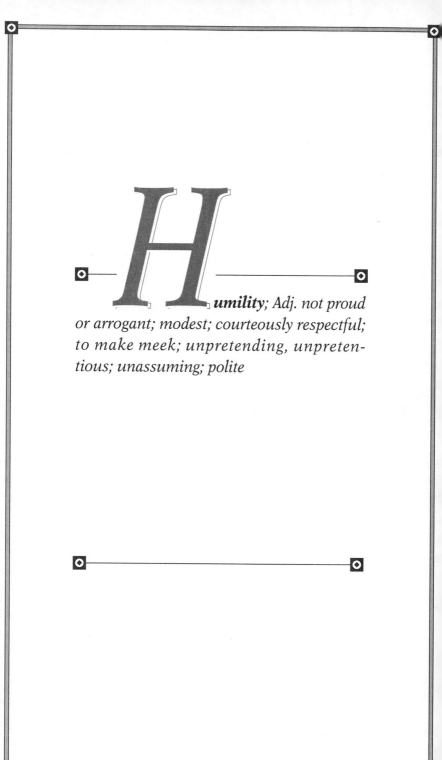

*H**umility**; Adj. not proud or arrogant; modest; courteously respectful; to make meek; unpretending, unpretentious; unassuming; polite*

BOASTING OF HUMILITY

Humility is just as much the opposite of self-abasement as it is of self-exaltation.
Dag Hammarskjöld

Years ago a game show called "Queen for a Day" made something of a contest out of misfortune. Housewives would compete to see who had the most tragic story, and the "winner" would receive a household appliance intended to make her life easier.

Some people take a similar approach to humility—treating it as some kind of contest. But as Hammarskjöld suggests, it sort of defeats the nature of humility to exhibit a "World's Most Humble Person" award in your trophy case. Yet, from the way some people carry on, you'd expect to find them wearing a cape with a big "H" on it, hoping others will take note of their "super" humility.

Actually, genuine humility is invisible. It's always much easier to tell who *isn't* humble. Self-exaltant and self-abasing people work much too hard to draw attention to *self*.

Humble people build others up, do the jobs no one else wants, and go about making the world a better place for everyone. They don't often get paid for it. Sometimes they don't get thanked. Maybe they don't even get noticed! Yet humility brings satisfaction to the lives of those willing to pursue it.

It might be your little secret that you're a humble person. But if you're going to keep secrets from other people, humility makes an excellent choice.

THE SAINT AND THE PAUPER

Humility has its origin in an awareness of unworthiness, and sometimes too in a dazzled awareness of saintliness.

S. G. Colette

*I*n *The Prince and the Pauper*, the title characters look alike and decide to trade places. The prince naturally learns humility from the harsh treatment he receives when he no longer has money or title. But the pauper discovers humility from the other extreme as he sees the responsibilities of a royal lifestyle.

The Colette quote relates humility to spiritual advancement. If we approach humility from a purely human level, we usually relate it to "unworthiness." It's the opposite of being "puffed up." But sometimes we go too far and distort what humility is all about. We resist taking pride in ourselves or our accomplishments. We even resist developing a positive self-image.

Yet we see ourselves quite differently when we realize that we are created in God's image. We have souls, minds, wills, and emotions. We have eternal value, and, though we fall far short of our potential, with His outside help we can be "dazzling."

The more we think about such truths, the more awed we become. It's not in realizing what we aren't that keeps us humble; it's in more fully comprehending what we *are and can become.* You are not a worthless pauper. You are a prince(ss) of a person. But that title has been given to you by Somebody else, so don't let it go to your head.

HUMBLE ABODES

Pride is the cold mountain peak, sterile and bleak; humility is the quiet valley fertile and abounding in life, and peace lives there.
Anne Austin

What a creative description of human qualities using geographic terms! Yet let's be clear—pride is not an entirely negative quality. When we look into the past, most of us should be able to see clearly several "mountaintop" experiences that stand above the terrain: marriage, graduation, promotions, a child's birth, or any number of other events. We have every right to recall those summits and the crisp air of accomplishment.

But a mountaintop is an inconvenient place to reside permanently. Not only is it "sterile and bleak," but it is most troublesome to get to where others live. People who reside on mountaintops have few friends who visit and tend not to get out often themselves. When planning a permanent residence, the "quiet valley" seems a much better choice. We can bear fruit in the warmth and the light and share it with others.

Surely you know people whose personalities reflect these two extremes. Some remain so proud that their heads are always in the clouds and they cannot function "down on earth." But humble people are "abounding in life." Other people are attracted to them.

Mountains look magnificent from a distance. And from time to time, they make a nice place to visit. But it is better to obtain the inner peace coming from identifying with others than the silence of being above the fray.

HUMBLE . . . AND PROUD OF IT

The Devil did grin, for his darling
sin is pride that apes humility.
Samuel Taylor Coleridge

The Screwtape Letters, a classic book by C. S. Lewis, is a tongue-in-cheek collection of writings from a senior devil (Screwtape) to his less experienced associate (Wormwood). After Wormwood's "patient" converts to Christianity, Screwtape advises:

> Your patient has become humble; have you drawn his attention to this fact? All virtues are less formidable to us once the man is aware that he has them, but this is specially true of humility. Catch him when he is really poor in spirit and smuggle into his mind the gratifying reflection, "By jove! I'm being humble," and almost immediately pride—pride at his own humility—will appear.

Sometimes humility seems like such a thankless characteristic. We replace whining with patience, aggression with self-control, and so forth. And the harder we try to be humble, the more we wish others would notice. But now that we're not as pushy, no one pays attention to us. That's where pride comes along. We either manipulate others to notice our humility, or we simply take excessive pride in ourselves and disdain lesser qualities in others.

But pride only apes humility, much as photographic negative reflects a picture. They have the same general appearance, but no one has any problem telling the difference. When we think we're passing off pride as humility, we're only fooling ourselves—and the devil does grin.

HUMILITY

Humility is just as much the opposite of self-abasement as it is of self-exaltation.
Dag Hammarskjöld

Humility has its origin in an awareness of unworthiness, and sometimes too in a dazzled awareness of saintliness.
S. G. Colette

Pride is the cold mountain peak, sterile and bleak; humility is the quiet valley fertile and abounding in life, and peace lives there.
Anne Austin

The Devil did grin, for his darling sin is pride that apes humility.
Samuel Taylor Coleridge

Integrity; N. soundness of and adherence to moral principle and character; uprightness; honesty

PLAYING IT STRAIGHT

*Nothing so completely baffles one who is
full of trick and duplicity himself, than
straightforward and simple integrity in another.*
Charles Caleb Colton

A favorite technique of many writers is to create fish-out-of-water stories, where a character is placed in a new and strange environment. One of these classics is Mark Twain's *A Connecticut Yankee in King Arthur's Court,* but most of us may be more familiar with "The Beverly Hillbillies" or the movie *Tootsie.*

Many of the assumptions we make about other people are based on what we know about ourselves. If you are a good-natured, fun-loving individual, you assume that most other people are too. But if you take a job in an aggressive and competitive office, you may soon learn differently. You don't have to change, but it sure opens your eyes to a world of different kinds of people.

If you are a sneaky, conniving, low-down person, "full of trick and duplicity," you are likely to find it next to impossible to deal with an honest and straightforward counterpart. You'll never believe a word the other person says because you're assuming lying is the only way to succeed in life. When offered a fair deal, you'll be suspicious. What's the catch?

There are lots of good reasons to become a virtuous person. If none of the others motivate you enough, you might consider being one just to keep people second-guessing you. Your handshake and spoken word will be enough to keep them shaking their heads.

A LITTLE KNOWLEDGE IS DANGEROUS

Integrity without knowledge is weak and useless, and knowledge without integrity is dangerous and dreadful.
Samuel Johnson

*P*erhaps you've known someone whom you might label a "know-it-all." Such people are usually quite intelligent, yet lacking in other crucial areas such as tact, sensitivity, humility, or perhaps even integrity. In life we should certainly seek knowledge, yet the mere accumulation of facts and truths is not enough.

You may think you're smarter than other people when you possess information they don't have. Without integrity, you might conveniently ignore those truths if it would benefit you. You might even use your knowledge to stay "one up" on them. But if you are a person of integrity, you do not take advantage of people. Integrity shares knowledge with others rather than hoarding it for personal gain.

No one wants to be ignorant. Ignorance of the speed limit will not keep you from getting a speeding ticket. But ignorance is not as bad as knowing the truth and intentionally acting in defiance of it.

The ideal solution is knowledge *plus integrity*. Knowledge alone can be good and beneficial. But if you don't have integrity as well, you don't know it all.

INTEGRITY

*Nothing so completely baffles one who is full
of trick and duplicity himself, than
straightforward and simple integrity in another.*
Charles Caleb Colton

*Integrity without knowledge is weak and useless, and
knowledge without integrity is dangerous and dreadful.*
Samuel Johnson

*J**ustice**; N. righteousness, equitableness, or moral rightness; the moral principle determining just conduct; the administering of deserved punishment or reward; guided by truth, reason, and fairness; agreeable to truth or fact; correct; in accordance with standards or requirements*

LAYING DOWN THE LAW

*Administer true justice; show mercy
and compassion to one another.*
Zechariah, Old Testament

*T*he newspapers or TV news occasionally relate odd rulings in court cases. Defendants charged with drunk driving are drunk *again*, but the judge says, "I don't want to ruin your life by putting you in jail, so you can go free." Vandals sneer at him, but he dismisses them because they're young. Similarly, he refuses to pass sentence on murderers or child molesters because they are victims of society. He justifies his actions by claiming that he is "merciful and compassionate." Would you agree?

Mercy and compassion are admirable qualities. God's message through the prophet Zechariah was to practice these virtues. But we must not overlook the other essential virtue: justice. Mercy and compassion cannot exist without some kind of fair and just system.

Actions have consequences, so people must be held accountable for what they do. In a court system, justice might require fines, community service, a rehabilitation program, or jail time. In our day-to-day lives it might involve punishing kids who misbehave, confronting a boss who shows prejudice, or becoming an advocate for abused women. Yet when the offending person shows genuine remorse for his actions (not just for getting caught), there is a need for mercy and compassion.

Sometimes you have to administer justice ("lay down the law"). But if, for every act of justice, you also add an act of mercy or compassion, you probably won't receive many complaints.

STRONG (AND FRAGILE) JUSTICE

Everywhere there is one principle of justice,
which is the interest of the stronger.

Plato

*P*erhaps you recall "Playground Justice." That's when a group of kids disagree about what to do, so they take a vote on it. Then, if the local bully expresses his discontent with the decision, they vote again—usually with a different result.

Or consider "Frontier Justice." In many cases the posse tracked down the suspect and hanged him on the spot when they caught him. Who needed courts or judges when a strong lynch-mob determined right from wrong?

In Washington, special interest groups and those with the most money prevail. Whoever is stronger on any particular day revels in victory while the other side complains.

"Justice" sounds like a powerful and even threatening word. Yet in its purest form, justice is quite fragile. It is easily perverted. The bullies, lynch mobs, and politicians of the world are quick to lay claim to it and "repackage" it for their own gain and at someone else's expense.

For justice to remain a virtue, we must cling to it in its purest form. We must have the same standard of treatment for everyone: friend and enemy, rich and poor, weak and strong. We will remember how we feel when we are treated unjustly and ensure that we never impose that feeling on anyone else—not if we can help it.

Are you a just person? You might be—if you're strong enough.

JUST WOLVES

*It is due to justice that man is
a God to man and not a wolf.*
Sir Francis Bacon

*R*ecently a decision was made to reintroduce wolves into the environment of Yellowstone National Park. They had once roamed freely there but had been killed off and run out. The decision was met with fierce opposition by area ranchers. The mere mention of wolves brought fear of missing livestock and other concerns.

Without a sense and system of justice, says Francis Bacon, that same fear would exist between people. Human beings are, after all, animals. Within each of us are instincts to survive and to come out on top in this wolf-eat-wolf world. Were it not for justice, many would not know where to draw the line.

Justice allows us to treat others more as God would. It is through justice that we all get fair and equal treatment, and those who wrongly persecute us are punished. It is good when other virtues (compassion, forgiveness, tolerance, and so on) accompany justice. But even in their absence, justice is a good foundation. The "eye for an eye and tooth for a tooth" system may not be the most God-like, but it is equitable and prevents retribution from escalating.

If you were on trial, you would prefer to throw yourself on the mercy of a just and godly court rather than being "thrown to the wolves." Try to remember that the next time someone else is in the same situation and you are the judge.

JUSTICE

*Administer true justice; show mercy
and compassion to one another.*
Zechariah, Old Testament

*Everywhere there is one principle of justice,
which is the interest of the stronger.*
Plato

*It is due to justice that man is
a God to man and not a wolf.*
Sir Francis Bacon

K*indness; N. friendly feeling; liking;*
— Adj. a good or benevolent nature or disposition; having, showing, or proceeding from benevolence; indulgent, considerate, or helpful; mild; gentle; loving

KINDNESS

KINDNESS IN RETROSPECT

That best portion of a good man's life,
His little, nameless, unremembered acts
Of kindness and of love.
William Wordsworth

*T*hink of the last funeral you attended. What was said about
the deceased? In the actual service, you probably heard of the
"significant" things the person did. But as people awkwardly
milled about to pay their respects, you probably overheard any
number of "little, nameless acts of kindness and love" performed by the person during his or her lifetime.

Surely Wordsworth didn't mean that *all* acts of kindness go
"unremembered." Many do. Others are recalled, but far too
late. At most funerals there is a sense of "I wish I'd told the person how much this or that act of kindness meant to me." In
most cases, people aren't remembered for heroic actions but
for the small, mundane deeds or words that showed how much
they cared.

A recent campaign has been waged to encourage people to
commit "random acts of kindness" to help offset the "random
acts of violence" we're more familiar with. The concept is a
good one, but it can only be successful if people are willing to
be "unremembered." Genuine kindness is others-centered; it is
rare because it must be performed with no desire of recognition in the present and no pride in the future. Yet for people
willing to do so, it's amazing how much difference one unexpected act of kindness can make in another person's life.

Each act of kindness is an investment. You may not be
around to see the dividends, but you can be sure they will
come.

131

SELF-INFLICTED BLINDNESS

Let me be a little kinder,
Let me be a little blinder
To the faults of those around me.
Edward A. Guest

*T*wo guys in Chicago recently became media "heroes" after being arrested for stealing a powerful purgative and "spiking" their boss's drinks for several days—a stunt they learned from the movie *Dumb and Dumber*. The woman's illness and embarrassment was a small consequence to their rise in becoming rock radio's "Dumb and Dumber Boys."

The rule in Hollywood seems to be, to attract the most people, shoot for the lowest common denominator. And the current trend is to *copy* such behavior. So how do we get beyond such a mind-set and seek instead the higher virtues?

The Edward Guest quote suggests an answer: blindness. Just as blinders on a horse's bridle eliminate its peripheral vision and keep it focused forward, we need to strap on blinders to stay focused on the needs of others while blinding ourselves to their shortcomings. Kindness requires a gracious attitude displayed in small but persistent actions performed whether the person "deserves" them or not. We should do them because that's the treatment we want from others.

By the way, the Guest quote was the source of the Glen Campbell song "Less of Me," written when popular songs could deal with issues such as gentleness and kindness. It's not such a dumb idea to pull out your LP record or 8-track tape and give it another listen.

NO ROUND TRIPS

I shall pass through this world but once. Any good thing therefore, that I can do, or any kindness that I can show to any human being, let me do it now. Let me not defer it or neglect it, for I shall not pass this way again.

Stephen Grellet

Suppose you're a filmmaker and your producer has arranged to demolish a thirty-five-story building in one of those breathtaking implosions to use in your movie. When you go to shoot the fall of the building, how much attention do you give it?

Even though the building's collapse will take only a few seconds, your planning will probably be careful and thorough to ensure that you capture the shot on film at every conceivable angle. Why? Because you won't get a second chance.

Yet when it comes to treating other people with kindness, we tend to act as if we have all the time in the world. But from the moment we're born, we begin to die. (Our buildings begin to collapse.) Each day, each hour, each second should be precious to us. We won't ever get that time back.

Tomorrow, approximately six thousand Americans will die. Do you think most of them are looking back and wishing they'd spent more time building up their reputations, demanding bigger raises each year, or chasing other selfish pipe dreams? Not likely. If we are to avoid those same regrets, we must start *now* to ensure that our priorities are what we want them to be.

We all know which road is paved with good intentions. Let's not waste any more time before turning around and taking a road less traveled. It could make all the difference.

KINDNESS

That best portion of a good man's life,
His little, nameless, unremembered acts
Of kindness and of love.
                    William Wordsworth

Let me be a little kinder,
Let me be a little blinder
To the faults of those around me.
                    Edward A. Guest

I shall pass through this world but once. Any good thing
therefore, that I can do, or any kindness that I can show
to any human being, let me do it now. Let me not defer
it or neglect it, for I shall not pass this way again.
                    Stephen Grellet

L ove; N. a feeling of warm *personal attachment or deep affection, as for a parent, child, or friend; affectionate concern for the well-being of others; the object or thing so liked; the benevolent affection of God for His creatures; tenderness, fondness, warmth, passion, adoration, devotion all mean a deep and enduring emotional regard*

GOOD INTENTIONS VS. REALITY

Love is, above all, the gift of oneself.
Jean Anouilh

A child admires his father and wants to be just like him, yet Dad is always busy and has some excuse not to spend time with his son. When Dad retires, he craves time with his son. But by now the son has a family of his own and is too busy. As it turns out, he's become just like his Dad.

This is the story line of Harry Chapin's song "Cat's in the Cradle"—as well as the lives of far too many fathers, sons, mothers, daughters, and friends in modern society. If love is truly the gift of oneself, it seems to be sorely lacking. We can't seem to find time to share our deepest longings and dreams. Sometimes our absence at important events is conspicuous.

That's not to say we don't try to make up for our lack of personal appearances. We send flowers, gifts, and cards. We try to help others meet financial needs. We may even plan elaborate vacations or cruises for the ones we "love." But, in most cases, what they would prefer is our face-to-face companionship and a heart-to-heart discussion. That is what they yearn for, and it doesn't cost a cent, but the value of the gift of love is priceless.

When are you coming home, Dad? The tragic answer in the Chapin song was, "I don't know when." But a much better response is, "Right away. And we'll get together then."

LIGHTENING A BURDEN

I have decided to stick with love.
Hate is too great a burden to bear.
Martin Luther King, Jr.

*I*t is difficult to love certain people. It is also hard to maintain an intense hatred. But love is a much better choice—even from a purely self-centered standpoint. If you show love to others, you get some personal benefits from your efforts (perhaps not what you'd like or had hoped, but at least *something*). Yet if you consciously attempt to hate someone, you essentially give that person control over you.

Think of your last fight with a spouse or close friend. Tempers flare, words are spoken, and one of you storms out. With time, anger dies down and you feel better. But that's only you. The other person may still be seething. So when you get back together, you must initiate reconciliation or resume the battle. That's the point when you must choose between love and hate. If you choose love, you admit you might have been wrong, then enjoy the benefits of making up. But if you choose hatred, you sacrifice your own good feelings just to continue a senseless conflict.

If we take hatred to a larger scale (races, genders, geographic localities, religions), it claims even more control. We must contrive all sorts of ridiculous beliefs and opinions about others, and it does us far more harm than it does them.

Martin Luther King, Jr., had his enemies. He died promoting love and tolerance toward others. But at least he didn't have the burden of hate to contend with, and his life lightened the burden for many people.

UNBRIDLED RESTRAINT

*The love of a man and a woman gain immeasurably
in power when placed under divine restraint.*
Elizabeth Elliot

*N*o one likes to discuss *restraint*. The word itself conjures up images of straitjackets, prison bars, and shackles. To use the word in connection with love seems preposterous. When it comes to romance, we want love without limits . . . unbridled passion . . . ecstasy that knows no bounds. To consider not only restraint, but *divine* restraint, may be disconcerting. Yet how many failed relationships can you think of that resulted from lack of restraint in the early stages?

Suppose you are given a two-pound box of chocolates. The restraint of eating one or two pieces each day provides a pleasurable experience, gives you something to look forward to, and allows you to enjoy the gift over a long period of time. A lack of restraint—eating the candy in one sitting—only leaves you feeling sick and never wanting to see another chocolate as long as you live.

Relationships, even those between husband and wife, are always developing. They are like plants that need the right combination of ingredients in order to thrive. And, like plants, relationships need occasional pruning or dormant periods to maximize growth at the appropriate time. Such "restraint" allows them to "gain immeasurably in power."

If a practical level of restraint isn't involved—for the good of the other person if not oneself—then it isn't love. And it surely isn't divine.

LOVE ISN'T BLIND

*What does love look like? It has the hands to help others.
It has the feet to hasten to the poor and needy. It has
eyes to see misery and want. It has ears to hear the
sighs and sorrows of men. That is what love looks like.*

St. Augustine

*I*t is said that parents can often hear their own child crying even when the child is in a noisy nursery with other crying babies. Studies have been conducted in which moms correctly selected their own child's socks from a pile of a dozen or so, just from a faint scent. Spouses can spot each other across a crowded mall. And people are frequently capable of superhuman strength when a loved one is trapped or in danger.

Love stimulates and empowers the senses. It motivates people to really listen to each other. It has 20/20 vision when it comes to noticing the hurts and needs of others. It seems to have a mind and a will to act when everyone else is apathetic.

One of the challenges of life should be to expand the range of our "love radar." Instead of being able to hear just a few loved ones who are crying or see only the plight of those who are closest to us, we ought to sharpen our senses so that we can detect the needs of an ever-growing number of people. Love keeps reaching outward.

Augustine's description sounds suspiciously like a *person*. If love has hands, feet, eyes, and ears, that could be *you*. And if it isn't, why not?

LOVE

Love is, above all, the gift of oneself.
Jean Anouilh

I have decided to stick with love.
Hate is too great a burden to bear.
Martin Luther King, Jr.

The love of a man and a woman gain immeasurably
in power when placed under divine restraint.
Elizabeth Elliot

What does love look like? It has the hands to help others.
It has the feet to hasten to the poor and needy. It has
eyes to see misery and want. It has ears to hear the sighs
and sorrows of men. That is what love looks like.
St. Augustine

*L**oyalty**; N. faithfulness to commitments or obligations; faithful adherence to a sovereign or government, or to a leader, cause, or the like; devotion; constancy; connotes sentiment and the feeling of devotion which one holds for one's country, creed, family, friends, etc.; allegiance*

RELATIONSHIPS OF STEEL

Only the person who has faith in himself
is able to be faithful to others.

Erich Fromm

*F*or young boys growing up in the 1960s, few substances sounded more threatening than *kryptonite.* That stuff could kill Superman, and, if Superman was out of commission, what hope was there for Lois Lane, Jimmy Olsen, and the rest of us? It was heart wrenching when Superman's help was desperately needed by one of his friends, yet he was weakened by kryptonite and unable to respond. To our great relief, however, something always happened that distanced Superman from that horrible substance long enough for him to fly to the aid of his friends.

We learned from Superman that we all have weaknesses. If even he could be occasionally impaired from helping others, certainly our own level of loyalty might falter at times.

On airplanes, people are told that in an emergency they should first put on their own oxygen mask, *then* deal with their children. The procedure is also a good one for being a loyal friend: first take care of yourself, and you'll be better equipped to attend to the needs of others.

Life is filled with "emergencies," so we need to consider what things act as kryptonite on *us*, hindering our faith in ourselves and thereby preventing us from being loyal to others. Your "kryptonite" might be greed, self-centeredness, pride, or any number of weakening influences. Once we identify these things and begin to remove them, we may start feeling pretty super.

MEASURE FOR MEASURE

An ounce of loyalty is worth a pound of cleverness.
Elbert Hubbard

*I*t's a privilege—and for some people, maybe even an ego trip—to have clever friends. We can't all be Jerry Seinfelds, so we gladly settle for being Georges, Elaines, or Kramers. We enjoy being entertained and having our spirits lifted by being around people who are witty.

But people with clever friends also realize that wit is no substitute for loyalty. When someone is clever and popular, the magnetic personality attracts crowds—and the bigger the crowd, the less time for each individual. Many of us carry scars from long ago when a popular peer couldn't or wouldn't make time for us.

Consequently, some of the best friends you'll ever find are those who don't know a punch line from a punch bowl. They always seem serious, and they never get your jokes. But when you need serious help they'll be there for you. When you are sharing the depths of your despair, they will cry with you rather than make jokes to ignore the pain.

They say an ounce of prevention is worth a pound of cure. Both are important and worthwhile. It's just that a little of one is worth a lot of the other. So it is with loyalty and cleverness. But if you ever try to replace one loyal friend with a series of lighthearted remarks, you'll discover it takes much more than a sixteen-to-one ratio.

LOYALTY

Only the person who has faith in himself
is able to be faithful to others.
Erich Fromm

An ounce of loyalty is worth a pound of cleverness.
Elbert Hubbard

Morality; N. conformity to the rules of right conduct; moral or virtuous conduct; virtue in sexual matters; chastity; moral quality or character
— Adj. of, pertaining to, or concerned with right conduct or the distinction between right and wrong; ethical; expressing or conveying truths

THE PATH TO GREATNESS

*Moral education is impossible without
the habitual vision of greatness.*
Alfred North Whitehead

*H*ave you caught yourself doing it yet—that thing you hated so much as a kid? When you are trying to teach your children to be good, moral, upstanding members of society, they want to know why. And as your patience drains, your reply becomes, "Because I said so, that's why!"

It's not easy for children (or adults, for that matter) to comprehend the benefits of morality. Sometimes immorality feels better, is more profitable, can provide bigger thrills, is more convenient, and lets us do whatever our friends are doing. It's hard to convince our kids (or ourselves) to continue down that narrow path of moral accountability.

The secret, perhaps, is the inner vision of greatness. We must remind our children (and ourselves) that the truly great people who lived—heroes, saints, rulers—were moral people. We can also see countless instances where a single moral indiscretion *prevented* people from becoming great or led to the downfall of once-great people.

Our accomplishments in life are like bricks in a building. Moral integrity is the mortar needed to secure them. Without morality, the building, no matter how grand, is bound to fall.

Why do we need "the habitual vision of greatness"? Because we need heroes. Even as we grow to adulthood, we secretly aspire to be heroic. But only the "pain" of morality leads to the "gain" of true greatness.

HOW FUTILE A FOUNDATION

Moral collapse follows upon spiritual collapse.
C. S. Lewis

Don't give your dogs whiskey in Chicago.
Don't burp or sneeze in church while in Omaha, Nebraska.
Don't walk down the street with your shoelaces untied in Maine.
If you're in Kansas, don't eat rattlesnake meat in public.

*T*hese are all laws still on the books in their respective locales. Decades ago when they were originally written, perhaps they served a useful purpose. Now they're simply something to joke about.

Similarly, a moral code of ethics quickly becomes antiquated when spiritual standards are abandoned. Moral principles are built upon spiritual ones. Once the spiritual rug is pulled out from under them, we lose our moral footing. Moral "laws" soon become little more than a joke.

Something within us wants to know why we ought to adhere to a strict standard when other people don't. If we are accountable to a higher spiritual power, the moral code makes sense. If not, it doesn't. The reverse is also true: we cannot solve moral problems until the spiritual void is filled.

Moral and spiritual commitment is not a choice everyone will make. But *you* can. And if enough people renew their commitment, they can slow the collapse. Who knows? They might even reverse the decline and bring order and fulfillment back to the world.

Skeptics say this will never happen, and there's one sure way to prove them right: don't try.

MORALITY

*Moral education is impossible without
the habitual vision of greatness.*
Alfred North Whitehead

Moral collapse follows upon spiritual collapse.
C. S. Lewis

Obedience; N. the act or practice of obeying; dutiful or submissive compliance; complying with or submissive to one in authority; yielding, deferential, respectful

THE SILENT WHEELS

He who yields a prudent obedience,
exercises a partial control.
Publilius Syrus

*T*eachers know it. Managers know it. Anyone who works with groups for any amount of time quickly learns this lesson. While the squeaky wheel might get some grease, the wheels that keep rolling smoothly are going to get to carry more of a load in terms of responsibility, trust, control, and other things that matter.

People who insist on doing things their way all the time are difficult for leaders to tolerate. No statement is taken at face value. No command goes unchallenged. No request is prudently obeyed. Others in the group are forced not only to endure the constant questioning and bickering of the "squeaky wheel" but also to do the work that he or she avoids in the meantime. And it doesn't take long for the leader to start doing just the opposite of what the troublemaker wants to do.

Obedient and responsive people, however, earn the confidence of others. Then, if they feel strongly about something and make suggestions, they can usually be trusted to be correct and to follow through. They gladly (obediently) share the responsibility, and so they earn some control.

It's one thing to be heard. It's quite another to be listened to. And "prudent obedience" is often what makes the difference.

ROOM FOR SECONDS

The height of ability in the least able consists in
knowing how to submit to the good leadership of others.
La Rochefoucauld

*T*he movie *Amadeus* detailed the life of Mozart, but it was really the story of Solieri. Solieri was a musician for whom music was an outlet to express the passion and reverence he felt. He could not understand how a person as brash, hedonistic, and indulgent as Mozart could have such a gift. The movie ends with Mozart dead under suspicious circumstances and Solieri in an asylum.

They say the hardest instrument to play is second fiddle. There are few happy endings when we compete instead of working together with those more talented, wise, and gifted than we are. Many good organizations crumble because the "second banana" grows jealous or thinks he can do just as well on his own. So he starts a rival company or service. But whereas the two working together made a strong team, the separation and competition weakens them, and perhaps they both fail.

It is through good leadership that we are given what we don't possess. There's no need to suffer when the answer is as simple as seeking out trustworthy leaders and submitting our talents to them.

A second fiddle competing against the first sounds awful. But if it lays down a harmony line and stays in tune, they make beautiful music together.

OBEDIENCE

He who yields a prudent obedience,
exercises a partial control.
Publilius Syrus

The height of ability in the least able consists in knowing
how to submit to the good leadership of others.
La Rochefoucauld

Patience; N. an ability or willingness to suppress restlessness or annoyance in waiting; quiet perseverance; even-tempered care; composure, stability, self-possession; submissiveness;

— Adj. bearing misfortune, provocation, annoyance, delay, hardship, pain, etc., with fortitude and calm and without complaint, anger, or the like; quietly persevering or diligent, esp. in detail or exactness; having or showing the capacity for endurance

THE FACE OF PATIENCE

*Be patient with everyone, but above all with yourself.
I mean, do not be disturbed because of your
imperfections, and always rise up bravely from a fall.*
St. Francis de Sales

*L*ook at the following "success record" of Abraham Lincoln:

- Defeated in his first run for the state legislature
- Involved in two businesses that failed
- Lost two consecutive party nominations to Congress
- Failed to receive a desired appointment to be Commissioner of General Land Office
- Defeated in his first two campaigns for U.S. Senate

Yet Lincoln was patient and believed in what he was doing. And posterity has judged him as a superior president.

We learn to walk by getting up every time we fall. We learn to succeed the same way. Yet when we say "Nobody's perfect," most of us usually exclude ourselves, so the first step is to quit putting ourselves down. Once we develop patience toward ourselves, we find that patience toward others comes more naturally. Patience, as St. Francis implies, is an act of bravery.

In today's team-project business environment, patience with others is critical. Without it, do you think we would have walked on the moon? Could we have built the Empire State Building? Would the Sistine Chapel have such a magnificent ceiling?

If you stopped kicking yourself for every mistake and developed the patience to keep plodding ahead, just what do you think *you* might accomplish in the years to come? From now on, every time you look at the face on a penny or five-dollar bill, try to remember where a little patience can get you.

THE PEAK OF PATIENCE

Patience and diligence, like faith, remove mountains.
William Penn

*I*n the days before automatic milking machines, many dairy farmers used three-legged stools to position themselves beneath the cow to do the milking. The stools were portable, sturdy, and stable. Similarly, the three "legs" of patience, diligence, and faith can provide stability for whatever you attempt to do in life.

Faith provides direction and confidence. Diligence is proactive and keeps us working at the task at hand. Patience is more reactive, providing the internal mind-set needed to endure the obstacles and challenges you are sure to face. Patience is required for "seed planting": investing today in things that won't pay off for decades, beginning worthwhile (but very challenging) projects, committing to relationships (such as one's small children) that will require much more giving than receiving for a long time.

Your life can abound with diligence and faith, but without the third "leg" of patience, you will never have a firm foundation. So if you need a "mountain moving" amount of patience, consider giving your obstacles mountainous names: Mount Neverest. The Rocky Marriage Slopes. Mount Crying Baby. The Crabby Executives Range.

As you climb, use the support of faith and the momentum of diligence. Then the next time you patiently confront your obstacle, just let the people nearby wonder why you're humming, "Climb Every Mountain."

HURRY UP AND SLOW DOWN

*On every level of life, from housework to heights of
prayer, in all judgment and all efforts to get things done,
hurry and impatience are sure marks of the amateur.*

Evelyn Underhill

*H*ow many F's do you see in the following sentence? (Please
count only once.)

> FINISHED FILES ARE THE RE-
> SULT OF YEARS OF SCIENTIF-
> IC STUDY COMBINED WITH
> THE EXPERIENCE OF YEARS

Studies have been conducted using this exercise, and it's
amazing how many people miss the correct answer. We often
miss the details if we are in a hurry. True, the number of F's
doesn't really matter. But it does matter whether we are devot-
ing enough time to spouse, children, jobs, housework, and personal spiritual development. Rushing through a paragraph may
be just a symptom of rushing through a life.

So how does a person deal with the problems of "hurry and
impatience"? You start to slow down *now*. If you really believe
what you're reading, you'll put the book down and take the
time—right now—to map out a strategy for how to slow your
pace today. Tomorrow do the same thing, whether it's reading
appliance directions or seeking God. Expertise develops slowly.

It may seem boring or inconvenient. If so, welcome to the
world of *patience*. Get used to it. In time you should feel just as
big a "rush" from a healthy pace as you do now from rushing
around. (And if you missed one of the six F's in the opening
sentence, you *really* need to start right away.)

PATIENCE

Be patient with everyone, but above all with yourself.
I mean, do not be disturbed because of your
imperfections, and always rise up bravely from a fall.
St. Francis de Sales

Patience and diligence, like faith, remove mountains.
William Penn

On every level of life, from housework to heights of
prayer, in all judgment and all efforts to get things done,
hurry and impatience are sure marks of the amateur.
Evelyn Underhill

P*erseverance; N. steady persistence in a course of action;*
— V. maintain a purpose in spite of difficulty or obstacles; continue steadfastly; to persist in speech, interrogation, argument, etc.; insist; to bolster, sustain, or uphold

IT DOESN'T TAKE A GENIUS

Nothing in the world can take the place of persistence.
Talent will not; nothing is more common than
unsuccessful men with talent. Genius will not;
unrewarded genius is almost a proverb. Education
will not; the world is full of educated derelicts.
Persistence and determination alone are omnipotent.

Calvin Coolidge

A sophomore in high school was cut from the school's basketball team. He responded as many of us would: he went home and cried. Yet that's where many of us would stop. After being told we weren't good enough, we would quit and pursue other interests. But this student persevered. He carried other team members' uniforms for a season, just to stay near the game. And he eventually made something of a comeback. Perhaps you've heard of him. His name is Michael Jordan.

For Jordan, the talent was there, but what if the perseverance hadn't been? Not only would his life have been quite different, but millions of sports fans would have missed the thrill of seeing him play. And what do we lose each time scientists, or others who have genius, are too quick to give up?

It's not that "persistence and determination" are more important than talent, genius, and education. It's that a combination is needed. Thomas Edison said, "Genius is one percent inspiration and ninety-nine percent perspiration." You might want to do your own experiments to see what percentages of talent and perseverance work best for you.

But some degree of perseverance in our lives is essential. Otherwise, ignorance of what we might have accomplished may be the greatest tragedy. we're ever unaware of.

SHORT, BUT NOT SWEET

Oh, the little more, and how much it is!
And the little less, and what worlds away!
Robert Browning

For want of a point, the A was lost.
For want of an A, the course was lost.
For want of a course, the scholarship was lost.
For want of a scholarship, the education was lost.
For want of an education, the battle was lost.

*T*he old story about the "loss sequence" of nail-shoe-horse-rider-battle seems a bit archaic, so here it is updated. But little things still count more than we give them credit for. The smallest oversights can have dire consequences. And faithfulness to small details can pay off in ways we never expect.

Being *consistent* in doing "the little more" is important. If a doctor sees one more patient instead of one less during her three hundred work days this year, that's six hundred additional people she can help. Similar results are seen if we study an extra half hour, if we smile more frequently, if we give a bit more to people in need, if we devote a little more time to relationships. These slight additions *on a regular basis* make a difference in the quality of life—for ourselves and for others.

Success is achieved when we deal with our shortages as quickly as possible. So what little thing(s) will make a difference for you? And how can you employ perseverance today to begin to remedy the problem?

STAR QUALITIES

Obstacles cannot crush me
Every obstacle yields to a stern resolve
He who is fixed to a star does not change his mind.

Leonardo da Vinci

*T*he concept of basing our lives "on the stars" has changed considerably over the years. Today astrology is popular among people who like to think that the stars determine their destiny. But when da Vinci lived, stars were vital in a much more practical way. That's how people knew where they were. Stars provided guidance for travelers. Their patterns in the sky changed with the seasons, but they did so with consistency.

The clarity of stars in those days also reminded people on a regular basis of the vastness and order of the universe. As people looked out at the thousands of visible stars each night, it helped put their current "obstacles" in perspective. They saw that there were bigger things than themselves.

Today, as the stars remain hidden behind man-made clouds of smog and the haze of electric lights, we lose touch with our place in the universe. We begin to think *we're* at the center. Our problems, therefore, loom larger than they should. And our distorted view of them can hinder us from persevering toward worthy goals.

We need to reconnect to the stars. Go out tonight and wish upon one. Hitch your wagon to one. Catch a falling one. Above all, let your mind dwell on the things that are above and beyond yourself. As you do, your obstacles should shrink down to a manageable size.

[handwritten annotations: "Garbage", "Yes!"]

PERSEVERANCE

Nothing in the world can take the place of persistence.
Talent will not; nothing is more common than
unsuccessful men with talent. Genius will not;
unrewarded genius is almost a proverb. Education
will not; the world is full of educated derelicts.
Persistence and determination alone are omnipotent.
Calvin Coolidge

Oh, the little more, and how much it is!
And the little less, and what worlds away!
Robert Browning

Obstacles cannot crush me
Every obstacle yields to a stern resolve
He who is fixed to a star does not change his mind.
Leonardo da Vinci

***P**rudence; N. cautious practical wisdom; good judgment; careful forethought; discretion; regard for one's own interests; sober prudence in handling one's affairs*

DEAR PRUDENCE

The eye of prudence may never shut.
Ralph Waldo Emerson

*P*rudence is a word that seems to be declining in use. It made for a nice name in a Beatles song, and George Bush tried to bring it back. But the concept of prudence is suspect because no one wishes to be considered "a prude." Yet the synonyms Webster uses to define prudence are words like *wisdom, judiciousness, discipline, reason, skill,* and *shrewdness.* These are all positive qualities, so perhaps we need to give prudence another shot.

Prudence keeps us from being "caught sleeping." In ancient Rome, sleeping during one's watch was punishable by death. Similarly, if we allow "the eye of prudence" to shut, we place ourselves at risk. We need to be alert when others try to charm us with hypnotic suggestions, trying to convince us that "Your eye is getting sleepy." You've heard such comments:

- "Don't worry about it."
- "Oh, come on. Just this once!"
- "You're missing a great opportunity."
- "You've got to crack a few eggs to make an omelet."

Risk and opportunity should not be routinely ignored. But those are exactly the opportunities where prudence is most needed. Prudence is the eye you use to "look before you leap." Make sure it never shuts. You may still decide to take the plunge, but you'll be able to see the softest and safest places to land.

TO ACHIEVE THE POSSIBLE DREAM

'Tis the part of a wise man to keep himself today for tomorrow, and not venture all his eggs in one basket.

Cervantes

*T*he concept of prudence, as described by this quote, is illustrated in the story of the ant and the grasshopper. The ant worked hard all summer to build, gather food, and do other essential things. The grasshopper, on the other hand, took it easy. He "lived for today" and thought the ant foolish for missing out on his freedom during the glorious days of summer. But when winter came and life became more of a challenge, the ant could retire to the place he had built and eat the food he had laid away. The grasshopper had no such plan, and his future suddenly became bleak.

We usually think of planning for the future in *financial* terms, yet more is involved. Though we say we never know what the future holds, we do to an extent. If all goes *well*, it includes physical decline, emotional struggles, and other challenges. Today, while we're younger and stronger than we'll ever be, we need to prepare wisely for what is likely to happen.

It's interesting that Cervantes is the source of such a down-to-earth quote. His literary hero, Don Quixote, was the dreamer who saw windmills as giants and common people as noble. But Cervantes realized the importance of being practical. It's OK to dream the impossible dream. But if we even want to see it come true, we'd better get started now.

NO MONKEYING AROUND

*Tell not all you know, believe not all
you hear, do not all you are able.*
                          Italian proverb

*T*his proverb is little more than common sense. If you tell all you know, you quickly become a bore. Like Cliff Claven on "Cheers," you spout useless facts until people can hardly stand to be around you. You reveal things told in confidence. You make yourself vulnerable.

If you believe all you hear, you never have a proper perspective on life. When you believe the boasts of others, your self-esteem drops in comparison. When you believe flattery, your self-image is boosted, but only artificially. When you believe lies or gossip, you make bad decisions.

If you do all you are able, you never rest. There's always another option: visit another family member, watch that episode of "Masterpiece Theater" you've never seen, read another book, spend longer hours at work.

The key to a more reasonable and prudent life is setting priorities. You say what is important and relevant, and keep the trivia to yourself (unless you have an eager listener). You listen to the voices of wisdom and tune out the rest. And after you figure out what is most essential, *then* you act.

The three monkeys that demonstrate "See no evil; hear no evil; speak no evil" are a good model to remember. If we also ignore the senseless, useless, and mediocre things all around us, our caution allows us to concentrate on what's important.

PRUDENCE

The eye of prudence may never shut.
Ralph Waldo Emerson

*'Tis the part of a wise man to keep himself today for
tomorrow, and not venture all his eggs in one basket.*
Cervantes

*Tell not all you know, believe not all
you hear, do not all you are able.*
Italian proverb

*P*urpose; N. the reason for which something exists or is done, made, used, etc.; an intended or desired result, end, aim, goal; determination; resoluteness; practical result, effect, or advantage

LIVING ON PURPOSE

Life, to be worthy of a rational being, must be always in progression; we must always purpose to do more or better than in time past.
Samuel Johnson

*I*magine your lifestyle if you had lived a century or so ago. Heating and cooking would require chopping trees and stacking firewood. Today you flip a switch. Water had to be drawn from a well or hauled from a spring. Today you turn a knob. Transportation required feeding and caring for horses. Today you twist the ignition switch and then push a button to adjust windows, mirrors, or music preference.

We appreciate the time-saving conveniences of modern life. But is this true progress? We have the time to do *more*, but are we doing *better*? Society in general doesn't seem to be improving. So Samuel Johnson's quote raises some questions: "What am I doing to make this world a better place?" and, "What is my purpose?"

Are we reading the classics to improve our minds? Do we develop our hidden artistic, musical, or other talents for the benefit of others? Do we reach out to those who are less fortunate? If you tried, you could probably list dozens of ways that you—yes, you—could make the world a better place. (If not the whole world, at least the world around you.)

"More" isn't necessarily "better." Do we have the drive and commitment to bring true progress to the world around us? Or is our purpose in life merely to consume the luxuries our progress has helped create?

GET SERIOUS

He who would make serious use of his life must always act as though he had a long time to live and must schedule his time as though he were about to die.

Emile Littre

*T*om Sawyer had the rare opportunity to attend his own funeral. Most of us won't have that privilege, but how would you like to write your own obituary? Rather than having a grieving family or an apathetic reporter try to come up with the right words to describe you, wouldn't *you* rather determine what is said?

To an extent, we do determine what is said about us after we die. If we want others to remember us as kind, giving, loyal, and faithful, we must start *now* to be that kind of person. If we do, that's what others will remember about us. If not, they'll be forced to come up with something else.

The Littre quotation reminds us that life is a marathon, so we must pace ourselves for the long haul. Yet each day is something of a sprint. We need to focus our energy on what counts today—always remembering that we must run again tomorrow.

Too often we reverse the process. We schedule important things as if we have forever to get them done, and we plunge into daily busywork as if the world will end if we don't get that last call made or form filed. A *serious* life finds the balanced perspective.

If, after you die, others can say that every day you did what was most important, won't that make a wonderful legacy and eulogy?

PURPOSE

Life, to be worthy of a rational being, must be always in progression; we must always purpose to do more or better than in time past.
Samuel Johnson

He who would make serious use of his life must always act as though he had a long time to live and must schedule his time as though he were about to die.
Emile Littre

*R*esponsibility;   Adj.
answerable or accountable, as for something within one's power, control, or management; involving accountability; chargeable with being the author, cause, or occasion of something; having a capacity for moral decisions; capable of rational thought or action; able to discharge obligations or pay debts; reliable or dependable; competent; honest; capable; trustworthy

RESPONSIBILITY

GIFT EXCHANGES

*From everyone who has been given
much, much will be demanded.*
Jesus Christ, New Testament

*I*n days past, people got water from pumps that had to be "primed." A jar of water sat beside the pump. The operator would pour in the water while pumping the handle, and water would come gushing out. You could take all you wanted, then refill the jar for the next person. Only a rude or ignorant individual would drink the water in the jar or neglect to refill it, leaving nothing for the next person.

Jesus reminds us of a similar principle. What we have been given is to be passed along to others. The more we have, the more we can offer.

This is true on numerous levels. The more financial assets we accumulate, the more we can invest in worthwhile enterprises. The more we know about God, the more spiritual maturity we can share. But on the most basic level, we ought to "give" our talents, abilities, and gifts to others. Your "gift" may be listening, singing, or a mechanical skill. If you have abilities that other people don't, it's your responsibility to share them. Response is the key.

In this age of recycling, we need to think in terms of recycling our talents. When we pour ourselves into the lives of others, like water into a pump, we may be surprised to see how much good is produced. It's something to get pumped up about.

A GREAT JOB EXCEPT FOR THE OVERHEAD

A great leader never sets himself above his
followers except in carrying responsibilities.
Jules Ormont

*D*ionysius, ruler of ancient Syracuse, had an attendant named Damocles, who made a naive comment about the ease and happiness of royal life. In response, Dionysius invited Damocles to be guest of honor at an elaborate feast. Damocles was proud to be shown such favor as he sat at the head of the table surrounded by food, drink, and entertainment. But during the evening he happened to glance upward and his joy quickly came to an end. Right above his head was a heavy sword, suspended by a single hair.

The point of Dionysius's object lesson was that with leadership comes responsibility. The joy of leadership is delicate, at best. Good leaders realize that they are no better than any of their followers; they simply have a different job description. And good followers realize they are just as accountable for success or failure as their leaders.

Good leaders never stop being servants. They may be out in front of other people, but it should be to set the example and take the brunt of opposition. They *lead* the charge into battle rather than *sending* others to do the "dirty work." So whether you're a leader or a follower—or perhaps both—first determine what responsibilities *you* should be carrying today. Then carry on.

RESPONSIBILITY

ONE POTATO, TWO POTATO

*Responsibility, n. A detachable burden easily
shifted to the shoulders of God, Fate, Fortune,
Luck, or one's neighbor. In the days of astrology
it was customary to unload it upon a star.*

Ambrose Bierce

"*I* didn't do it!"
"It was like that when I got here."
"Don't look at me!"
This could be dialogue written for Bart Simpson, but these statements are unfortunately all too common in families, workplaces, and other places where people try to dodge responsibility or pass it off on someone else. The Bierce quotation is tongue-in-cheek, yet the truth it reveals is quite serious.

These days, watching people deal with responsibility is like watching kids play "Hot Potato." The blame bounces from person to person, with no one willing to "lose." We blame parents, peers, circumstances, genetics, society, fate, and anything else that comes to mind. When we can't think of anything better, we have the all-encompassing "act of God" category as a last resort.

These things may indeed influence us, yet as individuals we each have the right and the power to make our own decisions—and the responsibility to live with the results. We need to resist the temptation to pass the buck, but rather let it stop with us whenever we should.

Yes, blame is like a hot potato. If you pick up a hot potato, your fingers might get burned a little. But it won't kill you. It's not even too hard to swallow. In fact, with a little seasoning and a bit of buttering up, it won't even leave a bad taste in your mouth.

RESPONSIBILITY

*From everyone who has been given
much, much will be demanded.*
Jesus Christ, New Testament

*A great leader never sets himself above his
followers except in carrying responsibilities.*
Jules Ormont

*Responsibility, n. A detachable burden easily shifted
to the shoulders of God, Fate, Fortune, Luck,
or one's neighbor. In the days of astrology it
was customary to unload it upon a star.*
Ambrose Bierce

*R**everence*; N. a feeling or attitude of deep respect tinged with awe; veneration; the outward manifestation of this feeling; a gesture indicative of deep respect; esteem; honor

GOING UP?

All real joy and power of progress in humanity depend on finding something to reverence, and all the baseness and misery of humanity begin in the habit of disdain.

John Ruskin

*I*n a word-association test, *reverence* might be connected to words such as *religion, God, respect,* and so forth. Yet a more basic definition might simply be "appreciation." "Finding something to reverence," then, can be as simple as showing an ongoing appreciation for art, music, architecture, or great literature.

Many people show no appreciation for such things. They respond with "disdain." For whatever their reasons, the refusal to show reverence begins a downward emotional spiral leading to a life of "baseness and misery." The inability to *see* things of beauty and loveliness initiates the inability to *feel* beautiful emotions.

On the other hand, if we appreciate the beautiful things around us, the emotional spiral is upward rather than downward. We discover "real joy" and the "power of progress." Our minds and spirits are lifted to new levels, toward something greater than ourselves. This is perhaps why reverence is so often connected with God and religious concepts.

A little appreciation can make a big difference in your life. Each time you see the beauty of nature, the display of creativity, or something else that deserves your reverence, you have an opportunity. It's like being on an elevator. You have only two choices. If you respond with reverence, you go in one direction. If not, you go in the other. And *you* decide which button to push.

GREAT EXPECTATIONS

Reverence is a good thing, and part of its value is that the more we revere a man, the more sharply are we struck by anything in him . . . that is incongruous with his greatness.

Max Beerbohm

*O*ne of the biggest compliments you hear about individuals today is that they are "great people." The phrase usually sums up character, personality, attitude toward life, and much more. It takes a lot of time together before we're ready to give such a glowing recommendation to someone else, and by then we usually overlook their little quirks that might be annoying to other people.

As you get to know others, you begin to understand them. You discover that their biting sarcasm was partially what helped them get through a previous prolonged sick spell. Shyness and timidity may have resulted from being abused as a child. Apparent oversensitivity to injustice might have come from a wartime experience. We see that these traits aren't necessarily *incongruou*s or out of character but are exactly the things that make them such "great people." We can show them reverence (respect) because what they've been through, good and bad, contributes to who they are.

The problem is that we're pretty selective about our friends. Sometimes we get beyond the things that offend other people. In most cases, however, *we* are the ones put off by quirky behavior. That's why "reverence is a good thing." If we can have a stronger respect for others, we'll get past the things that seem so annoying at first.

The world is filled with great people. But without the virtue of reverence, we're going to let most of them get away.

REVERENCE

---◇---

All real joy and power of progress in humanity depend on finding something to reverence, and all the baseness and misery of humanity begin in the habit of disdain.
John Ruskin

Reverence is a good thing, and part of its value is that the more we revere a man, the more sharply are we struck by anything in him . . . that is incongruous with his greatness.
Max Beerbohm

---◇---

S*elf-control; N. control or restraint of oneself or one's actions, feelings, etc.;*
— V. to exercise restraint or direction over; dominate; command; to hold in check; curb

A SELF-CONTAINED BATTLE

*I count him braver who overcomes his desires
than him who conquers his enemies; for the
hardest victory is the victory over self.*

Aristotle

Walt Kelly's cartoon opossum, Pogo, must have been a disciple of Aristotle's. His most repeated quote is, "We has met the enemy, and it is us." In the Bible, the apostle Paul was vocal on this point as well: "What I want to do I do not do, but what I hate I do" (Romans 7:15).

What kind of bravery does it take to fight an enemy? It's a natural instinct! You meet with opposition and you fight back. If you fight hard enought, you win.

But developing self-control is much more difficult. It's not instinctive. Your instincts are to do whatever you want regardless of consequences to others—again, to win. Victory in this battle with yourself involves confronting your most vulnerable secrets—meeting "the real enemy," so to speak. This commitment to total exposure requires courage because for most people it will result in the outpouring of lust, greed, jealousy, hatred, and a whole Pandora's Box of other things we've worked so hard to keep hidden.

These vices are enemies that will win out over self-control every time—until they are brought into the open and dealt with. Victory is possible. Self-control is achievable. But until we become brave enough to do battle with our inner desires, we don't have a fighting chance.

QUALITY CONTROL

How shall I be able to rule over others, [if I]
have not full power and command of myself?
François Rabelais

Would you seek help from a weight-loss counselor who weighed 250 pounds? A marriage consultant who had been divorced three times? A pastor who had been caught in an adultery scandal?

Using the Rabelais quote as justification, your first response would probably be, "No way!" If these people showed callous personal disregard for the principles they were promoting, you would be wise to look elsewhere for help.

Yet we know from personal experience that self-control is difficult. What if the weight counselor previously weighed four hundred pounds and was still losing? What if the marriage consultant admitted making mistakes early in life, but his fourth marriage was still going strong after thirty years? What if the pastor had genuinely repented and found forgiveness? Wouldn't these people have something worthwhile to say?

It takes time to develop self-control. We all make mistakes along the way. Although we don't want to blindly follow someone who can't keep his or her own life in order, neither do we want to be too quick to judge someone based on incomplete assumptions.

By all means, use your head when it comes to following the advice of others. But also use your heart to forgive their previous slips. Self-control is not a once-for-all decision. It is a daily struggle. And whether we lead or follow, we need to be understanding.

SELF-CONTROL

*I count him braver who overcomes his desires
than him who conquers his enemies; for the
hardest victory is the victory over self.*
Aristotle

*How shall I be able to rule over others, [if I]
have not full power and command of myself?*
François Rabelais

S*elf-knowledge; N. knowledge or understanding of oneself, one's character, abilities, motives, etc.; acquaintance with facts, truths, or principles, as from study or investigation*

SELF-KNOWLEDGE

FROM HERE TO THERE

*It is not enough to understand what we ought to be,
unless we know what we are; and we do not understand
what we are, unless we know what we ought to be.*
                                                    T. S. Eliot

J. Alfred Prufrock was a forlorn character living in a cultural
wasteland. He did not really understand himself or the world
around him. The modern world questioned any absolute meaning or standards, so Prufrock didn't know what was expected.

Thomas Becket was an archbishop during the Middle Ages.
He had an absolute standard of moral integrity that surpassed
the shifting politics of the day. He paid for it with his life.

Becket knew who he was and what he ought to be, though he
perished. Prufrock did worse; he succumbed to a shallow existence. Both of these characters, one fictional and the other his-
torical, are found in Eliot's poetry and drama. They represent
his personal quest for self-knowledge, a journey that went from
doubt to faith.

Are you asking the big cosmic questions—who you are, why
you're here, and what is required of you? Or are you suscepti-
ble to the latest advertising sound bytes with their shifting
standards of conformity? In order to attain the virtuous life,
begin by comparing yourself with the few Beckets rather than
the many Prufrocks. With knowledge, practice, and determination you can get there. If you can keep from getting yourself
killed by jealous rivals, you should turn out to be a person of
deep and lasting character.

TAKE A CLOSER LOOK

Self-reflection is the school of wisdom.
Baltasar Grácian

*M*any secrets of personal success are contained in two little words: "So what?" Every time you learn something new, you need to ask yourself this question in relation to yourself. For example, the quotations contained in this book are filled with mind-stretching, eye-opening wisdom. If your response is "That's nice," you won't get much from the accumulated knowledge of the original authors. But if you ask yourself "So what?" and try to apply the quotations to your own life, you will soon be a star pupil in "the school of wisdom."

Self-reflection leads to self-knowledge. You discover where the "holes" are in your life and focus on the areas that need the most time and energy. Otherwise, you tend to avoid the very things that need your attention.

It's like going on a diet. At first you hate to look in the mirror. But avoiding mirrors doesn't make you thinner. In fact, the more you focus on the excess weight, the more motivated you become. Then, as you devote yourself to a diet and exercise regimen, mirrors become more friendly. You see results, so you keep looking closer.

If you've been avoiding self-reflection for similar reasons, isn't it time to take a closer look? The more you work at it, the better you're going to like the person you see in your inner mirror.

SELF-KNOWLEDGE

It is not enough to understand what we ought to be, unless we know what we are; and we do not understand what we are, unless we know what we ought to be.

T. S. Eliot

Self-reflection is the school of wisdom.

Baltasar Grácian

Self-sacrifice; N. sacrifice of one's interests, desires, etc., as for duty or the good of another; the surrender or destruction of something prized or desirable for the sake of something considered as having a higher or more pressing claim

SELF-MADE INVESTMENTS

*Was anything real ever gained
without sacrifice of some kind?*
Arthur Helps

*T*hink back and try to recall those who had a positive influence on you—a teacher who regularly spent extra time to help you keep up, a Scout leader who taught you life skills, a church youth director who helped you feel good about yourself as a teenager (when you really needed it), an older business person who mentored you.

Perhaps at the time it seemed that these people were simply doing a job—and maybe they were. But in retrospect, you may see that they were willingly sacrificing time, money, or other resources for *you*. Perhaps the job was a thankless one for them. But now, years later, you realize how much their efforts helped to shape you into a terrific person.

If it's not too late, you might want to call or write a note of thanks to the people who have come to mind. Without them, you might have nothing "real" to show for your life today. After you've done that, perhaps you can think of several ways that a few simple sacrificial actions on your part might help shape another generation.

Your sacrifices may not result in immediate rewards. It might be several decades before someone recalls one of your sacrificial actions with fondness and appreciation. But won't that be a wonderful tribute when it comes at last?

THE LAYOUT OF LOVE

*Greater love has no one than this, that he
lay down his life for his friends.*
Jesus Christ, New Testament

*L*ove requires sacrifice. Great love requires great sacrifice. Most of us like to think we are capable of the "greater" love that Jesus described. If our kids were in a burning building, we'd go in to get them. If a spouse was attacked, we would try to take the assailant's bullet instead. But how many *friends* would you sacrifice yourself for?

Most of us aren't ready to consider the *greatest* degree of sacrifice. We need to focus instead on the thousands of ways we miss (or reject) *basic* love. The possibility of laying down our lives for someone is unlikely. But what if the criteria for "greater love" were one of these instead:

- Turning off the game every time your child wants your attention.
- Sacrificing a promotion to spend more time in community service.
- Forgiving a parent or adult child for transgressions of the distant past.
- Using four hours of "your" time each weekend to develop or strengthen new friendships.
- You fill in the blank. (By now several specific opportunities should have come to mind.)

If we have trouble with these "little" sacrifices, why even consider "greater love"? If we can't "die a little" in *these* matters, we aren't likely to lay down our lives in crisis situations.

SELF-SACRIFICE

*Was anything real ever gained
without sacrifice of some kind?*
Arthur Helps

*Greater love has no one than this, that
he lay down his life for his friends.*
Jesus Christ, New Testament

Service; N. an act of helpful activity; help; aid;
— V. to render assistance; be of use; to be in the service of; work for; to render obedience or homage; to answer the requirements of; suffice; attend; aid

SERVICE WITH A SMILE

The ideal of service is the basis of all worthy enterprise.
Principles of Rotary

*C*an you remember when you could get full service at a gas station for no extra charge? For the cost of a tank of gas, a nice young person would trot out to pump the gas, wash your windows, check your oil, and see if you needed water for the radiator or air for the tires.

It's bad enough to lose the convenience of full service at a gas station, but we also seem to be losing service as a personal virtue. When *people* shift to a focus on self-service rather than attending to the needs of others, our entire society suffers. Yet service with a cheerful, helpful attitude seems to be as antiquated as full-service gas stations.

Be pleasantly surprised if you find that kind of service. But if it's not there, that shouldn't keep *you* from demonstrating full service to others. If you can remember "the good old days" when a friendly, service-minded person eagerly attended to your every need, perhaps you can show others how pleasant it feels. If so, you might be surprised at how quickly the practice begins to spread.

A HELPING HAND

They also serve who only stand and wait.
John Milton

A wonderful story tucked away in the Old Testament (in Exodus 17:8-15) tells how the Israelites were being led by Moses out of Egypt and toward the Promised Land. Along the way they ran into some hostile opponents, the Amalekites, and a battle ensued. Joshua, who was young and strong, was placed in charge of the Israelite army. Moses went up on a mountain to oversee the battle. When Moses raised his arms toward heaven, Israel would win. But when his arms dropped due to weariness, the Amalekites would start to win. So two other people, Aaron and Hur, stood on either side of Moses and held his hands up until Israel was victorious.

Perhaps you're a person of action, like Joshua. That's good, because the world needs more strong, moral people. Perhaps you're a deep spiritual person like Moses. That's a superb gift to possess, for spiritual leadership is a rare and much needed quality—especially in a time when this commodity is rare.

But maybe you don't do much except provide support for others. You too have a strategic role. Your name may not go down in history like the person(s) you support. (Who remembers Hur?) But if it weren't for people like you, the "big name" people could not accomplish a fraction of what they get credit for. Your acts of service are every bit as important as theirs.

So don't just stand there. Stand there and serve.

SERVICE

The ideal of service is the basis of all worthy enterprise.
Principles of Rotary

They also serve who only stand and wait.
John Milton

Simplicity; N. freedom from complexity, intricacy, or division into parts; plainness; freedom from deceit or guile; sincerity; artlessness; naturalness

THE LIFEBOAT TEST

The ability to simplify means to eliminate the unnecessary so that the necessary may speak.
Hans Hoffman

*F*rom childhood many of us are fascinated by "hidden picture" puzzles, where key objects are disguised within a much larger scene. If we keep working at it, we discover which lines are only there to confuse us, and by mentally eliminating them we find what we're searching for.

But as adults we tend to do just the opposite. We are accumulators, not eliminators. It doesn't take long to amass so much "stuff" that we're unable to enjoy the basics. The things of value seem to lose their worth. When that happens, we need to reprioritize.

One way is to carry everything you own into a rickety lifeboat and, as it sinks, toss off things that are dispensable. (This is the quick method. You'd be surprised how rapidly you can prioritize as the water comes gushing in.) But a better method is to deal with unneeded accumulations before they overwhelm you: What do you possess that you've outgrown, no longer use, or is only taking up space? What could someone else use more than you? What can you loan to others whenever they need it?

Soon you'll begin to see clearly what things *are* necessary—relationships, sharing, love, helping. Simplicity never seems as threatening in actuality as in theory. The same principle holds true for character qualities as well as possessions. The simple truth is that the best things in life are still free. But it may "cost" you some disposable items to discover the secret.

HARD-WON SIMPLICITY

There is a simplicity born of shallowness, and falsely so called; and there is a simplicity which is the costly outcome of the discipline of the mind and heart and will.

Arthur Ramsay

See Dick. See Dick run. Run, Dick, run.

If you want a quick lesson in simplicity, recall the books you used while learning to read. Your ability to read anything is a result of that simple presentation of the English language.

Yet some people stop being simple as soon as they are able. They complicate their speech just because they are "cerebrally capable of fathoming convoluted grammatical passages even when complicated by excessive verbosity and multisyllabic expressions." You see what happens. When they become capable of complex speech and vocabulary, they are no longer contented with clear and straightforward communication.

Simplicity as a lifestyle is also quickly abandoned by some. Ramsay reminds us that life need not be "shallow," yet it can remain simple. Just as some people uselessly complicate their speech, others needlessly complicate their lives.

Simplicity as a lifestyle is a discipline in the same way as dieting, working out, or spiritual meditation. It takes hard work and a clear focus. It requires the mind (planning), the heart (commitment), and the will (continual devotion). There's nothing easy or automatic about it.

If we've spent years entangled in the complexities of life, becoming simple can be quite difficult. Yet in time we discover that simplicity is the antidote to many of our problems: superiority, envy, workaholism, and much more. It's a simple truth, but one worth much time and attention.

SIMPLICITY

⬥

---

*The ability to simplify means to eliminate the
unnecessary so that the necessary may speak.*
Hans Hoffman

*There is a simplicity born of shallowness, and falsely
so called; and there is a simplicity which is the costly
outcome of the discipline of the mind and heart and will.*

Arthur Ramsay

⬥

Sincerity; N. freedom from deceit, hypocrisy, or duplicity; earnestness; truth, candor, frankness;
— Adj. genuine; real; pure; unmixed; unadulterated

WHAT YOU SEE IS NOT ALWAYS WHAT YOU GET

Sincerity is to speak as we think, to do as we pretend and profess, to perform what we promise, and really to be what we would seem and appear to be.

John Tillotson

*I*f you are ever lost in the desert, stumbling through the blinding sand and running out of water, think about sincerity. Why? Because you're likely to see a mirage. Out in the distance will appear what seems to be a delightful pool of refreshing, life-giving water. But the closer you get, the more disappointed you will be because the "water" is really the heat causing you to think that something is there.

Insincerity is also a lot of hot air that causes considerable disappointment in the lives of others. It's easier to deal with apathy or outright rejection because at least you know where you stand. But insincerity promises what it doesn't deliver.

As Tillotson asserts, people must link words with thoughts, professions with pretensions, promises with performances, appearances with actuality. Sincerity is the virtue that helps the outer person accurately reflect the inner person. It requires no special skill to exaggerate, pretend, promise, and make a good appearance. Yet to follow through with genuine character—every time—requires a deep commitment from a sincere heart.

Anyone who has suffered from thirst and then "sees" an oasis knows the intense letdown of discovering it is just a mirage. But that disappointment is nothing compared to "seeing" what you think is a friend, only to discover later that it was only the mirage of insincerity.

WHAT'S YOUR POISON?

Sincerity is no test of truth—no evidence of correctness of conduct. You may take poison sincerely believing it the needed medicine, but will it save your life?
Tyron Edwards

*D*o you live next to someone you would describe as quiet, unassuming, and sincere? If so, be on your guard, because this is the usual response when reporters interview the neighbors of the latest psycho-killer. People are capable of doing horrendous things, yet be "good neighbors" without revealing their true nature.

Most people are good at "covering up" who they really are when they're around other people. With a bit of practice, alcoholics can hide most of the signs of their drinking. People who are harsh to spouse and child can be terrific colleagues at work. And it is quite common to "put on a front" around others to try to appear better than we really are.

In some cases our efforts are intentional. Yet as Edwards suggests, other times we are genuinely misled. The types of "poison" vary. In the twisted thinking of psycho-killers, their victims truly ought to die. Yet we deceive ourselves in many lesser extremes when it comes to virtue. Living together is accepted as a valid alternative to chastity. Aggressive competition replaces humility. Unwarranted suspicion leaves no room for trust. The "medicines" we take to cope with life may do us more harm than good.

When the medicine you've taken turns out to be poison, don't panic. A return to virtue—in all sincerity—usually serves as a sufficient antidote.

SINCERITY

Sincerity is to speak as we think, to do as we pretend
and profess, to perform what we promise, and really
to be what we would seem and appear to be.

John Tillotson

Sincerity is no test of truth—no evidence of correctness
of conduct. You may take poison sincerely believing it
the needed medicine, but will it save your life?

Tyron Edwards

***Temperance**; N. moderation of self-restraint in action, statement, etc; self-control; habitual moderation in the indulgence of a natural appetite or passion, esp. in the use of alcoholic liquors;*
— Adj. not excessive in degree as things, qualities, etc.

BIG GIFTS, SMALL PACKAGES

*Temperance is simply a disposition of the
mind which sets bounds to the passions.*
Thomas Aquinas

*K*ids usually like to receive large packages for birthdays and
Christmas. But sometimes they are disappointed when a great
big box holds a small and insignificant gift. On the other hand,
they are overjoyed when a smaller package is found to be
stuffed full of something they desire. A similar lack of emotional restraint usually disappoints us as grown-ups. But, if we
set limits and then pack all the passion possible within those
limits, we are seldom sorry.

Temperance is the virtue that "sets bounds to the passions."
This is another of the virtues, however, that seems to have
fallen by the wayside. If we think of temperance at all, it's usually in regard to the Temperance Unions of the late 1800s,
when Carry Nation and others stormed saloons with hatchets
to discourage drinking. It's not exactly a positive image.

But if we think instead of tempered steel, we can see that
temperance is a treatment to make a strong substance even
stronger. Temperance does to our desires what tempering does
to steel.

You might have a passion for fudge, for exercise, for travel,
for romance. But if those passions have no boundaries, they
will eventually weaken you instead of making you a better person. Yet if you temper these things by enjoying them to the hilt
within reasonable boundaries, that's a gift to yourself for which
you won't be disappointed.

FREE AND NOT-SO-EASY

*Freedom is not procured by a full enjoyment
of what is desired, but by controlling the desire.*

Epictetus

Since the 1960s, people seem to have developed a distorted perception of freedom. The "do your own thing" philosophy sounds good in theory but does not work in practicality. Historically, freedom is associated with war more than with peace and with disciplined control rather than with reckless abandon.

When the American colonists determined to become free from the persecution of England, they fought and died for liberty. They sat down and wrote a Declaration of Independence to affirm that freedom. Then they wrote an even longer document, the Constitution, to provide some *rules* for living in their new, free society.

In the years since, freedom has been maintained by wars, volunteer efforts, tax dollars, and other sacrifices. Freedom isn't free. It has a price. We can't always have what we desire. When you're late for an appointment, you may want to hit all the green lights. But you don't have the "freedom" to run through the red ones.

Temperance is placing self-imposed red lights on our desires that aren't in the best interests of others, or even ourselves. Personal freedom must defer to group freedom. We get what we pay for. Even though the price of freedom is temperance, it's still a good bargain.

TEMPERANCE

*Temperance is simply a disposition of the
mind which sets bounds to the passions.*
Thomas Aquinas

*Freedom is not procured by a full enjoyment
of what is desired, but by controlling the desire.*
Epictetus

Tolerance; N. a fair and objective attitude toward those whose opinions, practices, race, religion, nationality, etc. differ from one's own; freedom from bigotry; a fair and objective attitude toward opinions and practices which differ from one's own; interest in and concern for ideas, opinions, practices, etc. foreign to one's own; a liberal, undogmatic viewpoint; the act or capacity of enduring; endurance;
— Adj. forbearing

MORE THAN TOLERABLE

Give to every other human being
every right that you claim yourself.
Robert Ingersoll

*J*esus' Parable of the Good Samaritan is a classic illustration of Ingersoll's definition of tolerance. A traveler who had been mugged by robbers was left "half dead" on the road. A local priest and another religious leader passed by without attending to him. But a Samaritan—supposedly a hated adversary of the injured man—stopped to offer physical and financial aid until the man was strong enough to go on his way.

We all are willing to help those we like and are comfortable around—even if it's inconvenient or costly. Tolerance, however, offers *"every* right" to *"every* other human being." That means accepting people who are very different from ourselves and who can't benefit us in the slightest way in return for our efforts.

Most of us realize there are times when we must tolerate the thoughts or beliefs of other people. But we tend to think of tolerance in passive terms. The Ingersoll quote, however, describes an *active* tolerance. "Give" is a command. Tolerance is something we should *initiate.*

Tolerance usually comes late in the development of virtues. First you struggle to develop courage, diligence, contentment, and other qualities you wish to possess. Then, in tolerance, you willingly bear with others who think or act differently.

Perhaps you can recall an instance when you appreciated someone else's tolerance. If so, consider Jesus' advice to His listeners: "Go and do likewise."

TOLERANCE

LIVE AND LET LIVE

*Tolerance implies no lack of commitment to
one's own beliefs. Rather, it condemns
the oppression or persecution of others.*

John F. Kennedy

*A*s this is being written, the nation is in shock over the bombing of the Federal Building in Oklahoma City. One suspect is still at large, causing fear of further violence. The suspect in custody shows no remorse—not even for the deaths of more than a hundred people (so far), many of them young children.

The tragedy in Oklahoma City demonstrates the importance of tolerance in a way that written volumes cannot communicate. Unfortunately, tolerance of various beliefs and opinions is disappearing. Most organizations and individuals need a larger dose of tolerance. They need to stop seeing those who hold opposing viewpoints as "the enemy."

Kennedy reminds us that tolerating other viewpoints does not compromise our own. No matter how strongly we feel, we do our cause no good by acting intolerant. In the extreme, that's how buildings get bombed, abortion doctors are murdered, people are killed because of the color of their skin or clothing. Tolerance moves in the opposite direction. It is the courage to defend the rights of those with whom you most vehemently disagree.

So know what you believe and don't compromise the truth as you see it. Express your opinions loudly and strongly if you must. But remember that your views are never the *only* perspective. Even if we don't agree with other people, tolerance allows us to at least learn something from them.

TOLERANCE

Give to every other human being
every right that you claim yourself.
Robert Ingersoll

Tolerance implies no lack of commitment to
one's own beliefs. Rather, it condemns
the oppression or persecution of others.
John F. Kennedy

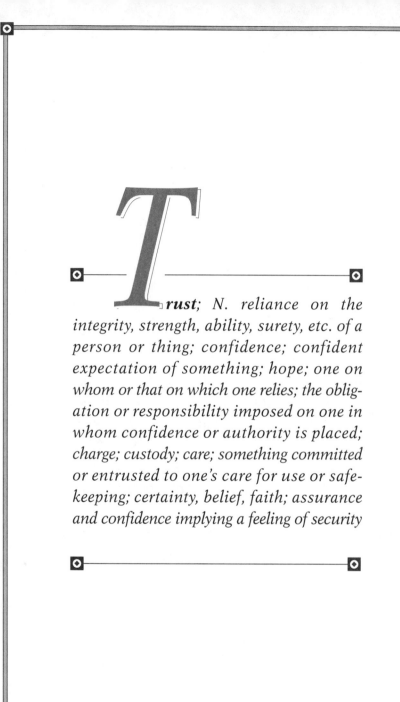

Trust; N. reliance on the integrity, strength, ability, surety, etc. of a person or thing; confidence; confident expectation of something; hope; one on whom or that on which one relies; the obligation or responsibility imposed on one in whom confidence or authority is placed; charge; custody; care; something committed or entrusted to one's care for use or safekeeping; certainty, belief, faith; assurance and confidence implying a feeling of security

TRUST

IN YOU WE TRUST

To be trusted is a greater compliment than to be loved.
George MacDonald

*G*enuine love is a key virtue, largely because of its nondiscriminatory nature. It pours outward toward all people, expecting nothing in return. Trust, on the other hand, cannot exist if something is not expected of the other person. Placing your trust in someone transfers responsibility for something you possess to that person. It is indeed a compliment to be trusted.

For example, a mother can love her children equally. Yet when it comes to trust, she knows which ones can be trusted to stay in the yard and which are likely to drift out into the street. A manager knows which employees will "run with" a project and which must be prompted, prodded, and watched over. And we all know which of our friends can—or can't—be trusted with money, secrets, pet care, and other responsibilities.

We should treat people equally. That's what love is all about. Yet trust is an *addition* to that equal treatment. Love should be freely given and received. Trust must be earned.

Trustwothiness is perhaps the most fragile of the virtues. Years of trust building can be destroyed by a single incident of letting someone down. We should give others the benefit of the doubt and, at the same time, be trustworthy. Can we be trusted to do so?

TRUST FROM THE INSIDE OUT

*A man who doesn't trust himself
can never really trust anyone else.*
Cardinal De Retz

*Y*ou hear a lot about "honor among thieves," but you rarely hear about them *trusting* each other. You've probably watched enough television detective shows to figure out how to get culprits to confess—you put them in separate rooms and give them time to get suspicious about each other. Mistrust works quickly, and it doesn't take long for one to "crack" and inform on the others in order to "cut a deal."

Thieves and other criminals "trust" each other initially because they need to work together to satisfy their mutual self-interests. But when the heat is on, the focus quickly becomes "me" rather than "us." Anyone who can't be trusted by law-abiding citizens cannot be trusted by his fellow conspirators, and ultimately can't even trust himself.

You can't offer trust to someone if you don't possess it yourself. So if you don't trust yourself, you must trust someone else to help you. That's not easy because we've all been hurt by people we have trusted. Yet when we search with discretion and care, we find many trust-building people willing to help make us more trustworthy.

Trust begins with ourselves, but it shouldn't end there. As your personal level of trust builds, remember that others are running in short supply. So first learn to trust yourself. Then pass it on.

TRUST

To be trusted is a greater compliment than to be loved.
George MacDonald

A man who doesn't trust himself
can never really trust anyone else.
Cardinal De Retz

Truth; N. true or actual state of a matter; conformity with fact or reality; verity; a verified or indisputable fact, proposition, principle, or the like; honesty; integrity; truthfulness; accuracy, as of position or adjustment; sincerity, candor, frankness; precision, exactness

TRUTH FANATICS

*They who know the truth are not equal to
those who love it, and they who love it
are not equal to those who delight in it.*
Confucius

H ow do you feel about basketball? Could you pass a test regarding the number of players on a team, number and length of playing periods, dimensions of the court, and basic playing rules? If so, you have a head knowledge of the game.

What if the TV volume were turned down? Could you provide the "broadcast" for the game yourself? If so, you know and love the game.

Finally, what if the test concluded by having you describe your own personal involvement in the game: How does it feel to hit the free throw that wins the game in overtime? What is it like to leap up and deflect the shot of your opponent? Or to stand behind the three-point line and watch the ball arc from your fingers and get "nothing but net"? Now you are immersed in the delight of the game.

But how you feel about the truth is more important than how you feel about a game. To know it, love it, and do it well requires a wider range of skills and a greater commitment than does a sport. When truth is at stake, the wins and losses count and the consequences continue long into the future. So don't be a mere spectator—become a fervent expert and play so that everyone will win.

You can *think* about truth all day long. But unless you're working up a sweat, enjoying yourself, and shouting "Yes!" every once in a while, you're missing out on a lot.

THE SIMPLE TRUTH

*The process of living seems to consist in coming
to realize truths so ancient and simple that,
if stated, they sound like barren platitudes.*

C. S. Lewis

A few years ago author Robert Fulghum wrote a best-selling book titled *All I Really Need to Know I Learned in Kindergarten.* His premise agreed with C. S. Lewis that truth is simple enough for anyone to understand. It's so simple, in fact, that it doesn't even sound significant.

We should be nice to one another. We should share what we own. We should be accountable to others besides ourselves. All these are simple truths that may "sound like barren platitudes." And, indeed, the mere knowledge of such truths is essentially worthless. Their *power* is discovered only when they are put into *practice.*

When you are kind to someone and later discover that your actions prevented his suicide, you've learned the power of caring. When you do what is right even when it is unpopular and feel great about yourself, another truth is revealed. When you sacrifice your own selfish desires in order to serve someone else and hear his gratitude, the deeper reality of truth hits like blinding sunlight.

What's the secret of converting truth from simplistic platitudes into vital realities? Lewis calls it the "process of living." Anyone can drift through life, but the secret is to create a meaningful path leading to integrity and wisdom. Other seekers have been discovering this path since ancient times and looking for companions along the way. Won't you join them in the search for truth?

TRUTH

THE GREAT DIVIDE

Truth—that long clean clear simple undeviable
unchallengeable straight and shining line, on
one side of which black is black and on the other white
is white, has now become an angle, a point of view.

William Faulkner

What is truth?

This question was asked during Jesus' trial, and it is still being bantered around courtrooms across the nation. Is murder wrong? Yes, usually. Yet defense attorneys try to convince juries that sometimes it is justifiable if the client was abused as a child, on drugs at the time, temporarily insane, in an extremely agitated state, acting out another of his multiple personalities, or whatever. All these things—and many more—have been used as defenses.

Our founding fathers considered certain truths to be "self-evident." Faulkner considered truth "clean," "clear," "simple," "undeviable," and "unchallengeable." But he also recognized the trend to reduce it to merely "a point of view."

Truth has no degrees and no detours. Something is true, or it isn't. Half-truths, as we've so conveniently named them, are lies. They belong on the wrong side of the "straight and shining line." We may *justify* half-truths, falsehoods, excuses, and such. (And if we can't, we can hire good lawyers who *will*.) But justifying them won't make them true.

So the question remains: What *is* truth? It may involve struggle to determine the answer in some cases. And it may be more difficult to act on our conclusions. But if you want your life to make sense, keep walking that straight and shining line.

TRUTH

◆

*They who know the truth are not equal to
those who love it, and they who love it
are not equal to those who delight in it.*
Confucius

*The process of living seems to consist in coming
to realize truths so ancient and simple that,
if stated, they sound like barren platitudes.*
C. S. Lewis

*Truth—that long clean clear simple undeviable
unchallengeable straight and shining line, on one
side of which black is black and on the other white is
white, has now become an angle, a point of view.*
William Faulkner

◆

Virtue; N. moral excellence; goodness; righteousness; conformity of one's life and conduct to moral and ethical principles; uprightness; rectitude; a particular moral excellence; a good or admirable quality, as of a person or some aspect of a personality; effective force; efficacy; power; a worthwhile attribute or property; goodness; potency; integrity

IF YOU CAN SET A PRICE, IT'S TOO HIGH

Few men have virtue to withstand the highest bidder.
George Washington

*I*s virtue a carved-in-stone principle that is always true? Or is it rather a "rule of thumb" to live by until a good enough reason comes along to do something else? Washington suggests that most people perceive virtue as something that's expendable—if the price is right.

A few years ago the movie *Indecent Proposal* had many of us discussing whether or not one act of adultery would be worth a quick million dollars. It's hard to fault the Demi Moore character for her decision when we are willing to "sell out" for so much less—cheating for a slightly better grade, demeaning co-workers to get ahead at work, lying to the IRS on our tax forms.

We are auctioning truth and faithfulness, reducing their value bit by bit, when we do such things. Can truly virtuous people even *consider* a price that would justify setting aside these principles even for a little while?

No. True virtue is priceless. As soon as a price is set, virtue is lost. And no potential gain can compensate for that loss. So as you begin to consider the value of virtue, ask yourself, "Do I know what I hope to gain by compromising my virtue?" And even more important, "Do I know what I stand to lose?"

VAIN IMAGININGS

Virtue seldom walks without Vanity at her side.
W. G. Benham

*F*ew experiences in life are as embarrassing as thinking that you look fine and suddenly discovering that something is amiss. You could have spent hours preparing to attend an important dinner. Makeup, cologne, clothes, and jewelry were chosen with great care. Every hair is be in place. But then, as you give your biggest smile to the guest of honor, everyone but you notices that enormous wad of spinach from your fettucini dish lodged between your front teeth.

We all can look foolish (and probably have at one time or other) without knowing it, even when trying to be at our best. Such events are the source of horror—and comedy. Likewise, as we become more virtuous, we can become too self-conscious of it—not out of embarrassment but out of pride.

There's nothing funny when Vanity secretly accompanies Virtue. It may be humorous to say "I'm humble and proud of it," but it is not entertaining to act that way. You will be more embarrassed than benefitted if Vanity is standing behind you, mocking every other Virtue you try to display. A little shallow pride is all it takes to overshadow the good qualities you work so hard to accumulate.

As we start down the road to a more virtuous life, let's check over our shoulders frequently to make sure we don't have an uninvited traveling companion.

THE PAY'S NOT GREAT, BUT THE BENEFITS . . .

Virtue is its own reward, but it's very satisfactory when Providence throws in some little additional bonus.

Woman's Home Companion

A man carries an old woman across a raging river. She turns out to be a goddess in disguise, who later rewards him.

An old man at a well asks a young girl for water. She grants his request and also waters his camels. As a result, she becomes a matriarch of the twelve tribes of Israel.

A couple invite their real estate agent to dinner. The meal prevents a diabetic reaction. *Twenty years later* they receive a five-figure bequest from the agent's will.

The first story is about Jason, leader of the Argonauts. The second is about Rachel, the mother of Jacob (Israel). The third is from a recent newspaper.

Such accounts capture our attention because we yearn to be rewarded for our virtue. Yet a virtuous life is seldom one of instant gratification. When it is, the bonus of Providence (divine benevolence) is usually intangible: inner peace, positive self-image, recognition by others. Still more bonuses may come in the next life, when they will count more than any crumb of gratification we might receive here and now.

We need a passion for virtue. It does have rewards—and bonuses. Just as Van Gogh kept painting even though he was unable to sell much while he was alive, we need to pursue virtue whether or not we see immediate perks. It *will* be worth the effort.

A PEACE OF YOUR MIND

Through virtue lies the one and
only road to a life of peace.
Juvenal

*E*dgar Allen Poe's story *The Tell-Tale Heart* confirms Juvenal's quotation. A murderer buries his victim under his house. When the police come to question him, the man begins to hear the beating of the dead man's heart. He assumes the police can too. He eventually breaks down and rips up the floorboards in a frenzied confession.

It doesn't take an offense as horrendous as murder to destroy peace. Doctors list symptoms—from anorexia to zits—that can be attributed to stress or some similar lack of peace. Migraines, ulcers, nights of insomnia, and more severe disturbances can be due to the shortcuts we try to take around virtue.

Peace is the product of internal harmony with yourself, others, and God. Genuine peace reveals itself at strange times: crisis situations, major conflicts, severe losses in life, and even at one's own time of death. This kind of peace comes from serving others, fulfilling your potential, and knowing that you lived a good life. Success, accumulation, competition, and similar goals are dead-ends on the road to peace.

A relatively new field of psychology is called integrity therapy. It is based on being true to one's conscience in order to find peace. The denial of personal integrity, it seems, is a source of psychological problems as well as physical ones.

In other words, virtue usually results in peace. Peace without integrity, however, is virtually impossible.

VIRTUE

Few men have virtue to withstand the highest bidder.
George Washington

Virtue seldom walks without Vanity at her side.
W. G. Benham

*Virtue is its own reward, but it's very satisfactory when
Providence throws in some little additional bonus.*
Woman's Home Companion

Through virtue lies the one and only road to a life of peace.
Juvenal

Wisdom; N. knowledge of what is true or right coupled with just judgment as to action, discernment, or insight; wise sayings or teachings; understanding; enlightenment

WISDOM

SHREWD INNOCENCE

Be as shrewd as snakes and as innocent as doves.
Jesus Christ, New Testament

Miss Marple is the stereotypical "little old lady" in a British mystery setting. She appears harmless and naive yet has a razor-sharp mind full of the awareness of human depravity. Her seeming innocence allows her to extract critical information needed by a crack detective.

The essence of wisdom is knowing when to be "innocent as doves." Certainly many situations in life call for a soft touch. Yet "innocent" people make easy prey. So the other part of wisdom is a shrewd hardness that makes sure we always keep our eyes open and our jaws clenched for an unexpected confrontation. We bear up during hard times and unfair situations, and we don't crumble when "the heat is on."

It's not easy to be snakelike and dovelike at the same time, yet wisdom demands that we play both roles. Wisdom allows us to soften when we *choose* to—not as a result of intimidation, scare tactics, manipulation, or other insincere efforts. At the same time, we can be just as tough as we need to be.

So as you prepare to confront the challenges of your future, strive for that odd combination of shrewdness and innocence. It will see you through a lot of life's mysteries.

GREEN WITH WISDOM

The seat of knowledge is in the head; of wisdom, in the heart. We are sure to judge wrong if we do not feel right.
William Hazlitt

William Hazlitt lived and died before the formation of 4-H Clubs, but he had the right idea. The four segments of the 4-H clover logo represent head, heart, hands, and health. Knowledge is valuable, but it deals only with the head. True wisdom requires that we take what we know and believe it with a passion (heart), put it into practice (hands), and make ourselves a better person because of it (health).

"Star Trek" fans know this to be true. Mr. Spock and Mr. Data are both individuals of profound knowledge, but they don't run the *Enterprise*. The wisdom of leadership involves much more than logical thought processes: qualities such as the instinct of second-guessing your opponent, emotion, commitment, intuition, and goodness. Wisdom is *applied* knowledge.

If you're looking for advice about a problem, would you go to someone with a photographic memory who could cite you paragraphs of answers from books, or would you prefer someone who can empathize with you because of similar life experiences? And when people seek *your* advice, do you respond with your heart as well as your head?

For some people, a four-leaf clover is simply a good luck charm. But from now on, let it serve as a reminder to use more than just your head in arriving at wise decisions and advice. When you do, your success will have nothing to do with luck.

SOAR LOSERS

*Wisdom is ofttimes nearer when
we stoop than when we soar.*
William Wordsworth

*W*hy do you suppose that kids have an almost inexhaustible thirst for knowledge, yet adults often lose that curiosity? Perhaps one reason is that we learn to drive.

In early life we play outside and have infinite questions about the things we discover: Why is the sky blue? What makes the grass green? What kind of insect just crawled in my ear? We walk, crawl, or skip to get from place to place. We have time to stop and stoop, smell and taste, poke and prod. We know our backyards better than anyone else. But soon bicycles allow us access to greater domains. We attain a wider span of information, but less depth. And by the time we learn to drive (to "soar"), the details are lost in a blur of speed.

There's certainly nothing wrong with soaring from time to time. But in most cases, the acquisition of wisdom comes from getting "up close and personal" with something or someone. It can't be done quickly or from a distance.

Buzzards can "soar" in circles all day and not learn anything more than where the latest dead animal is located. If we're looking for wisdom, we're likely to find it when we're a bit more down to earth.

PRESENT TENSE

Nine-tenths of wisdom is being wise in time.
Theodore Roosevelt

*T*oday you will receive 1,440 gifts. Each is exactly 60 seconds long. You will have to devote some of those precious gift-minutes to sleeping and eating. Your bosses, teachers, and other people in your life will provide firm direction about how to use others. Yet each day you can take whatever is left and do what *you* want to.

You can crash on the couch and watch a ball game that takes about 180 of your gifts, or squander hundreds more in further trivial pursuits. Or you can use some of them to gain knowledge and insight, build relationships with family or friends, or develop skills that will serve you well in a world of fast-paced change.

Roosevelt suggests that wisdom includes good time management—making every minute count. No one is saying that we should not occasionally slow down to smell the roses, watch a sunset, drive in the country, or otherwise enjoy life. But we should realize how precious these gifts are.

You've used one or two of today's gifts to read this page. But if you act on what you've read, perhaps those gifts will keep on giving.

WISDOM

○

Be as shrewd as snakes and as innocent as doves.
Jesus Christ, New Testament

The seat of knowledge is in the head; of wisdom, in the heart. We are sure to judge wrong if we do not feel right.
William Hazlitt

Wisdom is ofttimes nearer when we stoop than when we soar.
William Wordsworth

Nine-tenths of wisdom is being wise in time.
Theodore Roosevelt

○

Work; N. exertion or effort directed to produce or accomplish something; labor; toil; productive or operative activity; employment; the result of exertion; to act or operate effectively; to have an effect or influence, as on a person or on the mind or feelings of a person

BURIED TREASURE

*The world is sown with good: but unless I turn
my glad thoughts into practical living and till
my own field, I cannot reap a kernel of the good.*
Helen Keller

*I*f you found an old map that designated your backyard as the location of a buried treasure worth millions of dollars, what would you do? Most people wouldn't wait for the heavy digging equipment. They would rush out with picks, shovels, post-hole diggers, spoons, or whatever they could find to get beneath their perfectly manicured lawn.

Helen Keller tells us we need to "dig" in another sense, in which the payoff might be just as valuable. We must work to cultivate the good in the world. We like to indulge in "glad thoughts" about ethics, charity, and the like but never seem to get around to making them practical realities. Old-fashioned hard work is the key. We have to till the ground if we want to reap the desired crop.

In these days of supermarket selections, we've almost lost the concept of sowing and reaping. To plant seeds in early spring is to anticipate weeding, watering, and fertilizing. Why go to all that trouble? Because the reward of the harvest is worth it all. Kernels of good are all around us, yet we have to exercise sweat equity—do all within our power as individuals—in order to harvest them.

Goodness doesn't often grow without help. You might get some sore muscles and dirty hands in the process. But few things are as satisfying as tasting the fruit of the harvest after all your hard work. Evil thrives when good people do nothing. So start digging—you'll see growth sooner than you think.

FRINGE BENEFITS

Work spares us from three great evils:
boredom, vice, and need.

Voltaire

A dad agrees to coach a little league team. At first he dreads giving up his evenings and weekends. But then he begins to get back in shape by running around with the kids. He enjoys the fresh air and sunshine. He recalls his own carefree childhood. He is unprepared for these unexpected benefits, and they make the "job" seem more like a privilege.

Work can have multiple benefits. Many of us first approach the job market from the sense of need. Yet the surprise is that work also reduces levels of boredom and potential vice. Productive work is an ideal solution for kids who couldn't wait to get out of school, yet who complain of "nothing to do" before the first week of summer vacation is over. The activity of work itself combats boredom, and the responsibility involved helps to eliminate the temptation to get into trouble.

It is in the context of work that many virtues are honed: patience, loyalty, frugality, diligence, obedience. That is not to say that *every* job will bring rewarding results. But if one doesn't, we can look for another that will. Even finding the right job can be work in itself—yet the results are well worth the effort.

You don't have to be a Marine to discover that your work can be more than a job. It can also become an adventure.

WORK

The world is sown with good: but unless I turn my glad thoughts into practical living and till my own field, I cannot reap a kernel of the good.

Helen Keller

Work spares us from three great evils: boredom, vice, and need.

Voltaire

If as a result of reading this book you are interested in more information about how to integrate principles from the Bible with your life, please write to the following address:

Northfield Publishing
215 West Locust Street
Chicago, IL 60610